EQUALITY OR EQUITY

SERIES | **RACE** AND **EDUCATION**

Series edited by H. Richard Milner IV

OTHER BOOKS IN THIS SERIES

EQUALITY
OR EQUITY

TOWARD A MODEL OF
COMMUNITY-RESPONSIVE
EDUCATION

JEFFREY M. R.
DUNCAN-ANDRADE

Harvard Education Press
Cambridge, MA

Paperback ISBN 978-1-68253-747-3

Library of Congress Cataloging-in-Publication Data is on file.

Published by Harvard Education Press,
an imprint of the Harvard Education Publishing Group
Harvard Education Press
8 Story Street
Cambridge, MA 02138

Cover Design: Endpaper Studio
Cover Image: maginima/E+ via Getty Images

The typefaces in this book are Adobe Garamond Pro and Trade Gothic.

——CONTENTS——

──── FOREWORD ────

When I conceptualized the Race and Education Series for Harvard Education Press, I stressed the necessity for the series to highlight that studies, practices, and policies that advance race and education are exciting and yet disheartening, plentiful and yet scarce, interrelated and yet disparate. I sought to invite authors who are deeply committed to racial justice and action—not merely those interested in intellectual pontification without attention to ways to create emancipatory, transformative, and joyful educational experiences *with* young people in schools and classrooms. As I reflect on the contributions of the series, it has been essential that the units of analysis for the books shepherded readings through critical examinations of real issues that impact minoritized communities. In short, I wanted books to amplify what we know about race and education and also to bring innovative, empirically robust recommendations for transformative policies, practices, and research tools. To date, authors have addressed many of the topics I hoped they would, such as:

- Over-referral of Black and Brown students to the office to punish them for "misbehavior"
- Disproportionate suspensions and expulsions of Black and Brown students
- Serious effects of poverty on student outcomes
- Underrepresentation and under-enrollment of Black and Brown students in STEM areas

- Low numbers of Black and Brown instructors in the teaching force
- Underprepared educators who are unable to respond to Black and Brown students' needs
- Myths about the achievement and socialization of Asian American students
- Opportunity gaps across disciplines masked in the language of achievement gaps
- Unmet psychological, mental health, and socioemotional needs of Black and Brown students
- Narrowing of the curriculum that pushes out the arts and physical education in too many classrooms that serve Black and Brown students
- Unconceptualized and unactualized health services that address the needs of the whole child
- Poor collaborations and partnerships between schools and the families and communities they serve
- The cradle-to-school-to-prison pipeline and carceral system that ensnare too many Black and Brown students
- Misunderstood identities, needs, and expertise of Black and Brown students

In one single volume, Jeffrey Duncan-Andrade's *Equality or Equity: Toward a Model of Community-Responsive Education* addresses with breadth and depth several of the themes above. Grounded in his deep, rich, and diverse knowledge base, which he has developed from his own empirical studies across the world in classrooms and schools, Duncan-Andrade has produced a potentially revolutionary text. By *potentially revolutionary*, I mean that this book builds on the very best of what we already know (theoretically, conceptually) and how we know it (epistemologically) in the field of education, human development, sociology, psychology, epidemiology, and anthropology and pushes us forward with insights and strategies that can (and should) surely reframe curriculum, pedagogy, assessment, and relational interactions.

Indeed, Duncan-Andrade explains, "If we do not change *what* we teach, *how* we teach it, and *why* we teach it, then we cannot fairly expect outcomes to change for those children who find themselves perpetually disconnected from school." In this way, the book is about deeply understanding educators' inputs—that is, what they do—in order to identify patterns and trends in outcomes. We benefit from his wide, profound, and intense transdisciplinary knowledge as he theorizes community and cultural responsiveness as a necessary repertoire in working with and through contexts for educational ecologies that build self-knowledge, self-awareness, and critical hope with young people and adults alike.

As a foremost thinker, theorist, and researcher working at the intersections of race and education, Duncan-Andrade has written the book I wish I could have read as an early teacher of high school and community college young people. This book challenges as it teaches us!

H. Richard Milner IV
Cornelius Vanderbilt Distinguished Professor of Education
Vanderbilt University
Series Editor, Race and Education,
Harvard Education Press

CHAPTER 1

EQUALITY OR EQUITY

Which One Will We Feed?

"Not everything that is faced can be changed. But nothing can be changed until it is faced."

—James Baldwin, *I Am Not Your Negro*

When a prominent architect of No Child Left Behind (NCLB) revealed that under that policy, the educational opportunity gap for children of color and children in poverty had actually increased, the race was on to determine the next policy response to shore up a national education system that has perpetually failed to meet the needs of the nation's most vulnerable youth.[1] Common Core grabbed most of the major headlines, but in schools and districts serving youth of color and youth living in poverty, "equity" has quickly become a dominant theme. On numerous occasions, I have been called on to be a thought partner to support districts, schools, charter management organizations (CMOs), and policy groups as they work to develop their equity strategic plans. What has been particularly disconcerting for me in that work is the frequency with which the words "equality" and "equity" are being used interchangeably. We have never created schools that are equal, which on its face is an even less daunting prospect than creating schools that are equitable. Without truly understanding what equity means, how it is different from equality, and what that shift would mean for schools, the field will likely produce another jargony fad rather than a fundamental shift.

FINDING THE FOUNDATION

The first home my family bought in Oakland was a real "starter" home. There were serious structural issues with the roof, the flooring, the wiring, the plumbing, and the layout. Most of those issues were fairly visible at our walkthrough, even to the untrained eye. But when we received the report produced by the trained eye of a professional home inspector, we restarted our review with her examination of the foundation. Nothing was more important to us than her evaluation of the foundation because we knew that the other issues with the home, while costly to fix, would be a total waste of our investment of time and money if the foundation was not solid.

Discussions about remaking our public education system would do well to consider the fundamental importance of the foundation of our public school system. For over a century, US education has been doing what Tyack and Cuban called "tinkering toward utopia."[2] Over that period, schools *have* changed—often for the better. However, the impacts of these changes and improvements have disproportionately benefited middle-class and wealthier white communities. This is not to say that the experiences of working-class and poor children, children of color, and other socially and politically decentered groups have not also experienced some improvements in their school lives and outcomes. But any honest examination of the data in the aggregate reveals that the groups of young people who can least afford to fail in school have continued to do so in alarming and starkly disproportionate numbers to their whiter and more privileged counterparts.

A century of "tinkering" has not fundamentally impacted outcomes for all children because it has been just that—tinkering. Tinkering is what one does when looking to make small changes to a house well built. Our nation's system of public education was not well built. It is a system that, by its very design, was built to be unequal and segregated.

INEQUALITY BY DESIGN: A BRIEF HISTORY OF US PUBLIC SCHOOLS

The historical intent and purpose of public schools in the United States is well documented by educational historians.[3] Spring's *American Education*, now in its eighteenth edition, provides a thorough and well-respected examination of the origins and intent behind the public school project.[4] In it, he identifies the bedrock of the public school project as having three pillars (social, political, and economic), each pointing very much to the same end. Despite the "great equalizer" mythmaking about Horace Mann's common school project as the origin of public schools, a deeper historical treatment reveals a design that helps to explain many of the current inequities in our schools.

The worst-kept secret in the United States is that the overwhelming majority of public schools serving the nation's most vulnerable populations are the least resourced. The inverse is also true, in that the schools serving the nation's most affluent children are the best resourced. How can schools be the great equalizer, or an engine for the sustainable growth of a pluralistic multiracial democracy, if those who need the most get the least and those who need the least get the most? What we have created is a system of educational apartheid, which makes sense if we look at the historical origins, patterns, and purposes that undergird the educational house we have built.

An Equal Education System?

Equity and equality are *not* the same thing. *Equality* is defined as "the condition of being equal in quantity, amount, value, intensity, etc. The condition of having equal dignity, rank, or privileges with others; the fact of being on equal footing."[5] It seems almost absurd to propose an equal education system in a nation that has been so radically unequal since its inception. We are a nation that built much of its economic base on genocides committed against African people who were enslaved, brutalized, and murdered for their labor and Indigenous people whose land, culture, and lives were stolen. To build an "equal" education system in a society with this kind of historical investment in radicalized inequality and persistent, contemporary gaps in the "dignity, rank, and privileges" extended to people outside of the dominant culture seems reasonable only in a nation that aims to uphold systems of *in*-equality.

To give every child an equal education is not only dismissive of our historical and current forms of inequality, it is also misaligned with common sense and a century's worth of theory and research in child development and education. Differentiated models of curriculum and instruction date back to Dewey's *The Child and the Curriculum*.[6] So much of the work on differentiated approaches to teaching stems from commonsensical awareness that even in the most equal of circumstances, children will present with different needs and interests and the successful learning environment is one that is responsive to those differences.[7]

This is to say nothing of the fact that we have never seriously tried to create an equal education system in this country. Everyone knows that schools act as social mirrors. People who have the most in the broader society get the most in their schools, and those who have the least get the least in their schools. While a truly equal education system—one where every child literally got the exact same quantity of resources and quality of educational experience—would still produce unequal outcomes for some children, those gaps would likely be less stark if schools serving children in poverty had all the same resources as schools serving children of means.

Committed to Inequality: *Plessy, Brown,* and Legacies Not Undone

In a society that has historically been so unequal, how did we even start to have a conversation about equal education? The concept of a system of equal education is fairly new in the United States. As a national effort, it really begins with *Brown v. Board of Education* (1954), although state-level cases such as *Mendez v. Westminster* (1947) laid some important legal groundwork.[8] What is often overlooked in discussions about the *Brown* case is the fact that the *Brown* decision was necessary precisely because the US Supreme Court had previously legislated inequality with *Plessy v. Ferguson* (1896).[9] *Brown* is effectively corrective legislation to respond to *Plessy,* one of the most egregious decisions ever made by the court and the one commonly known to have "sanctioned the 'separate but equal' doctrine."[10] Thus, a pivot toward equity demands an examination of *Plessy's* relationship to *Brown* and the subsequent pursuit, promise, and problems of pursuing an equal education system in a national culture that remains deeply influenced by *Plessy.*

Under Plessy, the education system delivered on the separate, but not on the equal. Will writes that, before *Brown,*

> segregated black schools were under-resourced and underfunded compared to the white schools. In some places, black students were forced to travel long distances to school without provided transportation. Black teachers were often paid less than their counterparts in white schools, and taught with outdated textbooks that were handed down from the white schools in the district. Some of

the black school buildings were crumbling, with inadequate heat-
ing and cooling systems.[11]

Plessy normalized, in policy and law, the Jim Crow status of
youth of color in every public sector of the nation—and most notably for our purposes here, this includes the education system. It
established a policy structure that helped to build and maintain a
colonial model of education that largely remains with us today, one
that Watkins argues was designed to "control, pacify, and social-
ize subject people. [An education that] has always been inextricably
connected to state politics and the labor market."[12]

Along came the *Brown* decision, ostensibly to right this wrong.
But the court never acknowledged that *Plessy* was wrong. In fact,
Chief Justice Earl Warren's majority opinion on *Brown* was silent
on every aspect of *Plessy* except as it related to schools and only as it
related to children of color. One could speculate on a whole host of
reasons as to why the court chose not to explicitly overturn *Plessy*,
not to acknowledge *Plessy*'s long reach into all aspects of US life, and
not to consider *Plessy*'s deleterious impact on the social and cultural
sensibilities of white children and families.

Perhaps the court considered that the plaintiffs in the *Brown*
case were arguing against *Plessy* based solely on access to schools.
This might make sense if the *Plessy* decision was argued based on access to schools, but it was not. *Plessy* was about railcar access, and its
use was extended to schools. Warren even notes this fact in writing
the unanimous decision on *Brown*. He is very intentional throughout that decision to repeatedly qualify the *Brown* decision as one
related only to "the field of education." Somehow, the logic used in
Plessy that extended a ruling focused on transportation to create a
national culture of separate but equal in schools and other matters
of public domain did not apply to the *Brown* decision. *Brown*, despite its significance, was a half-measure; one that failed to use the

power of the court to reverse its own decision on *Plessy*, undermining its own Constitution's Fourteenth Amendment and reinforcing the white supremacist culture—so noxious to our pluralistic multiracial society—that remains embedded in every mainstream US social institution.

One might also speculate that the court thought it was breaking ground with *Brown*, finally hearing a case that would establish an important first step in the dismantling of *Plessy* altogether. But three years earlier, in a US District Court in South Carolina, Judge Waties Waring, issued a dissenting opinion that presented a scathing critique of *Plessy* (*Briggs, Jr., et al. v. Elliott, et al.* (1952)).[13] This case was one of the five cases Warren's Supreme Court considered in hearing *Brown*.

Judge Waring's opinion in the *Briggs* decision, particularly given the time in which it is written, is worth quoting at length here:

> [T]he humiliation and disgrace of being set aside and segregated as unfit to associate with others of different color has an evil and ineradicable effect upon the mental processes of our young which would remain with them and deform their view on life until and throughout their maturity. This applies to white as well as Negro children. . . . we must unavoidably come to the conclusion that racial prejudice is something that is acquired and that that acquiring is in early childhood. . . . If segregation is wrong then the place to stop it is in the first grade not in graduate colleges.[14]

Sadly, in his decision, Warren chose to cite a lower court ruling from a Kansas court, regressing the logic of Waring's decision:

> Segregation of white and colored children in public schools has a detrimental effect upon the colored children. The impact is greater when it has the sanction of the law, for the policy of separating

the races is usually interpreted as denoting the inferiority of the Negro group. A sense of inferiority affects the motivation of a child to learn. Segregation with the sanction of law, therefore, has a tendency to [retard] the educational and mental development of Negro children to deprive them of some of the benefits they would receive in a racially integrated school system . . .[15]

Warren's choice established an interpretation of desegregation that suggests it is beneficial only to children of color. In so doing, Warren failed to acknowledge what Waring clearly saw, which is that racial segregation is a scourge to the rule of law *and* the very fabric of a true democracy. It negatively impacts *all* children and, therefore, *all* communities stand to benefit from desegregated schools.

The *Brown* decision does not appear to address, let alone acknowledge, the fact that the white community is the most racially segregated in the nation and that this fact undermines the cultural development of white children to be able to fully appreciate, respect, honor, and engage the cultural diversity of our nation. *Brown* appears to be based on the court's belief that the real evil of segregated schools is that children of color do not get access to white children and white schools. In fact, Warren plainly states and answers the question that the court believes is in front of it: "Does segregation of children in public schools solely on the basis of race, even though the physical facilities and other tangible factors may be equal, deprive the children of the minority group of equal educational opportunities? We believe that it does."

Speculation for cause aside, *Brown* has been a failure. It has failed to racially desegregate schools and it has failed to put an end to unequal schools. In their report on the sixty-fifth anniversary of *Brown,* UCLA's Civil Rights Project concludes that schools, particularly those in the South and the West, have ignored *Brown* and have become increasingly segregated for the last thirty years. In the press release for the report, Gary Orfield, the report's lead author and codirector of UCLA's Civil Rights Project, is quoted as saying:

> As we mark its 65th anniversary, the promise of *Brown* appears a distant vision in our dangerously polarized society. Segregation is expanding in almost all regions of the country. Little has been done for a generation. There has been no meaningful federal government effort devoted to foster the voluntary integration of the schools, and it has been decades since federal agencies funded research about effective strategies for school integration. We have to do more.[16]

Jongyeon Ee, the report's coauthor, adds that "school segregation is not simply an educational issue that stands out in certain communities, or regions, but an imminent social issue that seriously threatens the cohesiveness of our nation. Segregation exacerbates our differences, fueling division and tension across our schools, communities and nation."[17]

This is not to say that *Brown* has been without impact. Although the nation has largely failed to deliver on the court's promise to desegregate schools, there have been a series of deeper and enduring structural impacts that emerged as unintended consequences of *Brown*. All of these impacts, some positive for previously segregated groups and others deeply troubling, largely resulted from the aforementioned failure of *Brown* to see segregation as a national crisis for all communities, rather than just as a crisis facing people of color.

White Innocence and Unintended Consequences

A full accounting of the impact of *Brown* reveals several significant unintended outcomes. Some of those outcomes moved groups closer to equity. Others have frozen groups out. Sadly, but perhaps not surprisingly, the latter groups are precisely the groups that *Brown* purportedly aimed to support. An assessment of the more positive unintended outcomes appears in a 2010 article by Jeffrey Goldberg, editor-in-chief of *The Atlantic*.[18] The article captures an email dialogue between Goldberg and Martha Minow on Minow's book *In Brown's Wake: Legacies of America's Educational Landmark*. At the time, Minow was dean of the Harvard Law School.[19] It is worth interrogating their discussion as it seems emblematic of far too much of our nation's historical relationship to, and present sensibilities about, racial and social justice.

The article, "The Surprising Consequences of Brown v. Board of Ed," discusses the positive "surprises" of *Brown*, but remains largely uncritical of the negative impacts of *Brown*. One would think that the dean of Harvard Law, arguably the most prestigious law school in the nation, would have a more profound expectation that the nation uphold a ruling from the highest court in the land and that the court would be bolder in its efforts to correct one of its most egregious decisions. The title of the article alone, not to mention the subsequent questions and responses from Goldberg and Minow, amount to what Gutiérrez describes as "white innocence":

> the rationalization of a legacy of racial discrimination and the overturning of a well-established legal precedent as an "Aha! Moment"—the "Who knew? moment" that 1) absolves historical discriminatory practices and beliefs, 2) provides the context for a redemptive move by the court, 3) preserves "white innocence" and the status quo; and, thus, 4) requires no fundamental structural change in the legacy of cultural, social, and institutional racism in the United States. As a consequence, there is no compelling moral obligation for the "innocent" to acknowledge and challenge the underlying logic of the inhumanity and inequity that fuels racism.[20]

Between them, Goldberg and Minow meet all four of these criteria. Criteria 1 and 4 are met when Goldberg concludes that "the
Supreme Court could ultimately not mandate true racial integration."[21] Minow concludes that law is "more like a fence than a spur
to inner change. Law is typically better at saying 'no' than at saying
'yes.'"[22] They absolve the court for its failure to explicitly renounce
Plessy, a decision that clearly said "yes" to a sweeping and deeply
toxic white supremacist policy, the legacy of which permeates our
nation's culture to this day. They give full pardon to a nation that
has been utterly recalcitrant to the law of *Brown* and the court that
devised it. In the end, neither presents any expectation whatsoever
for fundamental structural change to address the legacy of cultural,
social, and institutional racism in the United States.

While Minow does register "disappointment that public K–12
schools today are in most parts of the country racially imbalanced
in their enrollments," she jumps quickly to lamenting that *Brown*
was not given its due for "shattering the racial apartheid of Jim
Crow laws, [and the] racial hierarchy enforced by vigilante justice
and lynching [that] deprived African-Americans of access to public accommodations, good jobs, political participation, and more."[23]
"That era is over," she proclaims, rather than holding the court to
account for the legacy of Jim Crow, which was made all the more
possible and potent because of *Plessy*.

In the same year that Minow made these claims, Michelle Alexander released her book *The New Jim Crow*.[24] Minow offers little
criticism of the failure of the court's decision and subsequent enforce-
ment of *Brown* to register outcomes that advanced racial justice. She
states that the intent of her work is to "focus on these other realms
to do justice to *Brown* to reclaim the path it represents: people can
work together, using law and organizing socially and politically, to
change the opportunities and practices for all kinds of people"—

except, apparently, people of color. Minow's position here is naive at best and borders on apologist at worst. It is quintessential white innocence, preserving status quo sensibilities that institutions and systems of power are working just fine and that the nation is making sufficient progress to right the wrongs of our past.

Minow does name four unintended consequences of *Brown* that are not without importance in the movement for social justice in our society:

> 1) the advocacy for gender equality in public school that first took the form of seeking co-education but over time has taken the shape of policies supporting single-sex public education; 2) the push to "mainstream" students with disabilities—including students with mental disabilities so that they may attend part or all of the school day with other students; 3) the emergence of school choice, first as a device for avoiding court-ordered desegregation, then as a technique for encouraging racial desegregation, and then as a technique intended to promote competition and school improvement; and 4) the ultimately successful effort to secure constitutional approval for the use of public funds in support of private religious education.[25]

It seems that our nation has found the moral fortitude to draw on *Brown* to begin addressing all sorts of bigotry and discrimination, just not racism. In point of fact, there is one particular unintended consequence that did not make Minow's list and that has been largely ignored in the discussions about *Brown's* impact. Vanessa Siddle Walker documents the tragic destruction of Horace Tate, a Black Georgia principal whose career was strategically undone by the white administration in his district following the *Brown* decision.[26] Tate's case is that of thousands and thousands of Black teachers and school administrators in the wake of a *Brown* decision that saw integration in schools as a project of assimilation, leaving no use for Black educators in the project, as the benefit was for Black children to have access to white people and resources. There was no value for white children to have access to Black culture or Black educators. The Black principal and teacher pipeline was decimated post-*Brown*: "Prior to *Brown*, in the seventeen states that had segregated school systems, 35 to 50 percent of the teaching force was Black."[27] Present day, there is not a single state that is anywhere close to that number of Black educators. In fact, according to the National Center for Education Statistics (NCES) only 7 percent of public school teachers are Black and only 11 percent of principals are Black.

There is clear and widening research that indicates that student-teacher demographic matches have positive impacts on placement in gifted programs, test scores, overall academic achievement, teacher expectations, and reduced suspensions, expulsions, and detentions.[28] This alone makes the decline of Black teachers post-*Brown* a tragic consequence of a law that aimed to improve educational outcomes for children of color. But Gershenson et al. take our understanding of the significance of this loss of Black educators to another level with their finding that being exposed to just *one* Black teacher in elementary school has a massive impact on educational outcomes for Black youth generally, but particularly for Black boys living in poverty.[29] Their study took "mounting evidence of teacher-student demographic match effects on short-run, immediate outcomes such as test scores, attendance, and suspension" and examined long-run impacts on educational attainment such as high school graduation and college enrollment.[30] Using a massive data set that tracked cohorts entering the third grade between 2001 and 2005 in all public schools in North Carolina, they "conservatively estimate" that exposure to "at least one Black teacher in grades 3–5 significantly reduced the probability of dropping out of high school among low-income black males by . . . 39%" and increased likelihood of intent to pursue a four-year college degree by 19 percent among all Black students and by 29 percent for males.[31]

Stunned by the size of the impact revealed in their study and the gravity of the findings, they sought to test it in another state to insure validity. They found similar patterns in the state of Tennessee, showing "exposure to a same-race teacher results in higher graduation rates and greater likelihood of taking college entrance examinations. . . . Moreover, rather than self-reported college aspirations, the Tennessee STAR data provides arguably more objective measures of college intent, sitting for an entrance exam such as the SAT or ACT, which is a costly action." The researchers called this finding "striking" because the confirming data is from a different state and the means of identification is coming from a different source.[32]

Research that illuminates reasons for this effect is expanding and is discussed throughout this book, but most significant for the discussion in this section is the significance of the relationship between the massive decline of Black educators as a direct result of *Brown*. Not only did *Brown* fail to desegregate or equalize schools serving children of color, it had a doubly negative effect in that it decimated a significant Black educator force. Both of these effects can surely be traced to the fact that the *Brown* decision finds itself part of a legacy that thinks of white supremacy, racial justice, and social justice as problems whose resolutions lie solely in granting access to racist and classist systems of power to people of color. This is what has passed for "equality" in the equal education movement. The remedy was, and largely still is, to allow all children access to a white, male, middle-class, English-speaking, heteronormative system of education. This, the logic goes, would be "equal" because then everyone has the same chance to become as close to white, male, middle-class, and English-speaking, and heterosexual as possible. This sits at the heart of the relationship between white supremacy and schooling—a maintenance model for the most radically unequal modern democracy in the world—and it all but insures the preservation of the status quo and no fundamental structural change in the legacy of cultural, social, and institutional racism in the United States. It allows high-ranking scholars like Minow to inject what Martin Luther King, Jr., called the "tranquilizing drug of gradualism" into their analysis of our progress, providing evidence of exceptional individuals as proof that significant social and economic changes are underway and that the era of radicalized racial inequality is in the rearview mirror:[33]

> I did want to give *Brown* its due for shattering the racial apartheid of Jim Crow laws, where statutes and ordinances mandated segregation by race not only of school children, but also their textbooks in summer storage; and where racial hierarchy enforced by vigilante justice and lynching deprived African-Americans of access to public accommodations, good jobs, political participation, and more. That era is over, and the social movement surrounding *Brown* generating the 1964 Civil Rights Act and political and economic changes that at least in some measure contributed to the successes of people like Oprah Winfrey, Ken Chennault, and Barack Obama.[34]

Arguments such as these are dangerous. They maintain a corrupt and failing education system by ignoring massive amounts of evidence to the contrary in research from medicine, public health, economics, physiology, and social epidemiology that argue we have built a society that is socially toxic to people of color and virtually every other group that finds itself outside of our WASP-centric society and the "equal" school system that so powerfully maintains it.[35]

Black teachers pre-*Brown* were modeling success for students, but they also understood what it took to find that success in a racist and classist society. So, they were not just teaching the same reading, writing, and arithmetic that white children were receiving, they were teaching it in the context of being Black in a white supremacist society. This is not to say that white children should not also be exposed to these teachings, but they do not need those lessons to survive and navigate systems of power. White children do need these lessons if they are to play their part in their communities to be racial justice allies with communities of color and warriors against the legacy of white supremacy they inherit. But without these lessons, children of color will continue to be burdened with the task of drawing their own navigational map for the ever-changing terrain of white institutional power.

EQUITY AS THE SUPERIOR GROWTH MODEL

The pursuit of an equal education system under the yoke of this nation's history, both inside and outside of the institution of school, does not make sense at this juncture of our society. If we are truly committed to confronting and righting the wrongs of our past, then we must commit to the design and implementation of an equitable school system. Equity is defined, *concretely*, as "what is fair and right."[36] Few events in my life have made the difference between equality and equity clearer than the birth of my twin sons. For all intents and purposes, they are as equal as two children can be. Amarú, the "oldest" by about forty seconds, is constantly thirsty, so much so that by the time he was two years old, he had figured out how to relocate the step stool from the bathroom so that he could serve himself from the refrigerator's water dispenser. Taiyari, on the other hand, is constantly hungry, so much so that I have dozens of pictures of food morsels scattered across his shirts; presumably for later snacking.

I have the great fortune of traveling all over the world to give keynote lectures to educators, administrators, policy makers, and researchers as part of my work to support them as they disentangle the concepts of equality and equity. I often open my keynote by using this example from my sons. I show a photo of Amarú shoving a straw into the top of a coconut and adjacent to that photo is a picture of Taiyari with food littered across his collar. I then show them an image where both boys are given an identical bottle of water and I ask the audience: "Is this is equal?"

I have done this talk over a hundred times, on three different continents, and in any number of settings and venues. Without exception, someone in the audience shoots their hand skyward and with absolute certainty in their voice they shout out "No!"

"Why?" I ask.

"Because, one of your sons is thirsty and the other is hungry," they reply.

"What does that have to do with my question?" I shoot back.

This leads to any number of reactions from the respondent. Some folks double down and insist that it is unequal. Others stutter and backtrack. Still others attempt to change their minds as they realize where this is headed. I press on.

"You see, your problem [insert respondent's name] is that you changed the question because it's not the right question. You changed my question from "Is this equal?" to "Is this fair?" That is the correct question for us to be asking and the answer to that question is unequivocally 'no.' The problem, though, is that there is virtually nothing in the discussions about an equal education that talks about fairness."

The idea of an equal education system presumes a social, economic, and political reality that has never existed in these United States. It completely ignores centuries of radicalized inequality wrought by white supremacy, male supremacy, hetero-supremacy, class supremacy, and xenophobia. It ignores the fact that we are the only industrialized nation in the history of the world to have committed two genocides: the genocide of Indigenous people of this land and the genocide of African people via the institution of human enslavement. To be frank, it is absolutely absurd to talk about an equal education system in a nation that has spent nearly the entirety of its existence committed to insuring inequality among its inhabitants. On virtually every metric imaginable, the United States is the most unequal of all the developed nations in the world. Perhaps one day we will be ready for a conversation about an equal education system, but today is not that day.

This book aims to end debates that sit at the heart of national uncertainty about whether we should be committed to equality or equity for our children. How we go on this question dictates the destiny of our nation for every generation to come. This is not hyperbole. This debate sits at the heart of every policy discussion about education. It permeates decisions about funding, discipline, assessment, curriculum, authorization, and hiring. The decisions we make about what matters most in the education of our children literally sets the course to come for every element of our national agenda.

If we choose to make a commitment to educational equity, we need to understand that the pivot from an equal education system to an equitable education system is not a soft pivot. Equity is a hard pivot that will not be achieved without a much deeper understanding of the reasons equal education has largely failed to be Horace Mann's "great equalizer"; why equity is the superior model for a pluralistic, multiracial democracy; and what it would take for us to make it our priority.

CHAPTER 2

ON BEING DATA DRIVEN

"Don't play what's there. Play what's not there."

—Miles Davis

Schools and districts all over the nation are saying they want to be data driven as a core strategy of becoming more equitable. Despite the widespread uptick of this approach to educational reform, very little has changed for the most vulnerable students. This can largely be attributed to the fact that most schools are looking at outcome data rather than process data. Most of what we find in the improvement science research clearly indicates that effective systems change is not driven by outcome data.[1] Rather, meaningful institutional learning is the result of deep investments in process data (data that examines the processes and practices that produced the outcomes) and a commitment to innovate, fail, and learn at a much more rapid pace and in a much more collaborative fashion than currently happens in schools.

I was recently giving a talk to a school district in Seattle, Washington. Since I live in Oakland, California, I needed navigational assistance to get from my hotel to the event location where I was speaking.

I punched the address I was given into WAZE, which is my preferred navigation system. WAZE reads that address as data and uses that data to consider a whole host of factors in order to plot the quickest route to my destination. What if I had put in the wrong address? I would surely end up in the wrong place. But I still would have been data driven. It is not about being data driven, it is about being driven by the right data. If we keep ending up in the same wrong place with the same groups of students, then we need to change the data we are looking at if we intend to plot a more appropriate course with them.

SIXTY-FIVE-PLUS YEARS OF AN "EQUAL" EDUCATION SYSTEM: WHAT DOES THE DATA TELL US?

Educational Apartheid

Wide swaths of longitudinal data clearly reveal that our national investment in an "equal" education system has failed to produce a healthy nation state—in point of fact, on virtually every indicator used to measure the wellness of a society, the United States ranks at the bottom of the industrialized world, and we continue to trend in the wrong direction.[2]

Not long before Arne Duncan left office as the top education official in the nation, he was all over national media lauding our nation's progress on high school graduation as the best it has ever been. At the time, I was teaching high school English at Fremont High School in East Oakland, arguably one of the worst-performing high schools in the nation: our four-year matriculation rate hovered at around 60 percent, and our four-year college eligibility rate sat at around 2 percent. This is my neighborhood high school. It is the high school to which my twin boys will naturally matriculate. At the time of Duncan's announcement, I had been teaching in Oakland for nearly twenty years and it was my assessment that we were doing worse than ever. Listening to Duncan's claim left me with feelings of deep cognitive dissonance.

One of my problems is that while continuing along my journey as a classroom teacher, I also pursued my PhD, and as part of that pursuit I was trained in data collection and data analysis. This training brought me to a stark realization that all the displays of data that had been placed in front of me over the years as an educator were not actually data. They were interpretive displays of data that, when interrogated more deeply, revealed a clear and conscious decision to tell a very particular story about that data set. My training taught me that a skilled data scientist could take virtually any data set and tell you several different stories with it, depending on how they chose to display and narrate that data to their audience.

Further investigation of the data set about high school graduation reveals that our national trends are deeply troubling. When controlling only for parent income, the mapping of high school graduation in our nation's public school looks like a nearly perfect map of coast-to-coast educational apartheid (see figures 2.1 and 2.2).[3]

These graphics are striking displays of what everyone in the country already knows—namely, that those who have the most get the most in school and those who have the least get the least in school. In short, we have built a national public system under the guise of equality where the children who can least afford to fail in school are failing at catastrophic rates. No nation serious about a commitment to democracy can possibly sustain itself with data trends like the ones we are seeing in our public schools.

Economic Apartheid

Our nation's distribution of wealth, or lack thereof, over the last several decades is as troubling and apartheid-like as our high school graduation data (see figure 2.3).[4]

FIGURE 2.1 2013 Adjusted Cohort Graduating Rate for non-low-income students

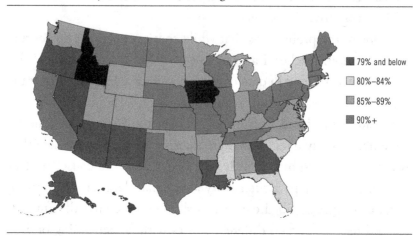

Source: Cision PR Newswire, https://www.prnewswire.com/news-releases/grad-nation-report-says
-us-on-track-to-reach-90-percent-high-school-graduation-rate-by-2020-300081602.html.

FIGURE 2.2 2013 Adjusted Cohort Graduating Rate for low-income students

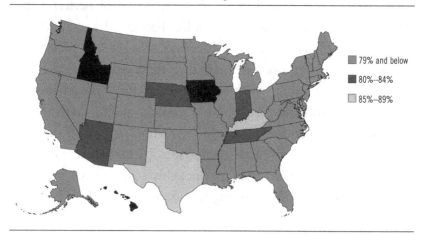

Source: Cision PR Newswire, https://www.prnewswire.com/news-releases/grad-nation-report-says
-us-on-track-to-reach-90-percent-high-school-graduation-rate-by-2020-300081602.html.

FIGURE 2.3 Share of national wealth in OECD countries*

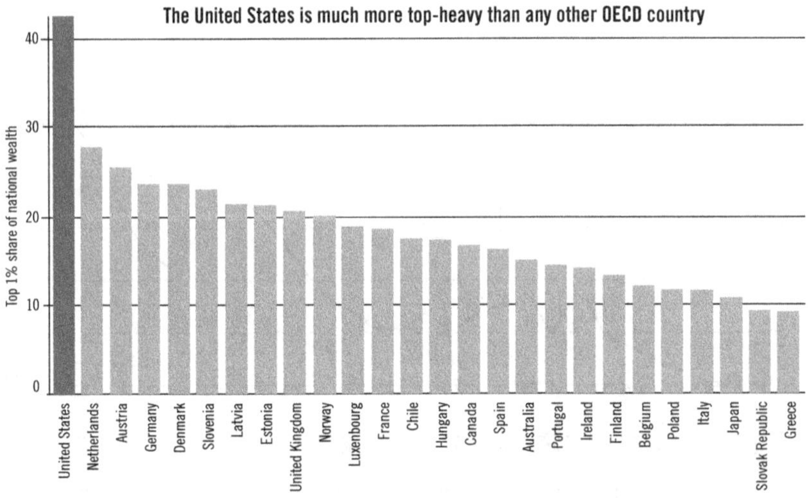

Source: OECD.
*2015 or most recent.

Research from Inequality.org, a project of the Institute for Policy Studies (IPS), reveals that the "top 1 percent in the United States hold 42.5 percent of national wealth, a far greater share than in other OECD countries. In no other industrial nation does the richest 1 percent own more than 28 percent of their country's wealth."[5] Economist and former US Secretary of Labor Robert Reich is deeply concerned about the fact that we have created one of the most unequal economic systems in the history of the industrialized world.[6] He argues that "of all developed nations, the United States has the most unequal distribution of income and we're surging toward even greater inequality."[7] Despite our "equal" education system, the past four decades have spurred a rocketship-like ascent in income for the top 1 percent (+281 percent), while the middle fifth and bottom fifth have grown just 25 percent and 16 percent, respectively (see figure 2.4).[8]

FIGURE 2.4 Income gains at the top dwarf those of low- and middle-income households

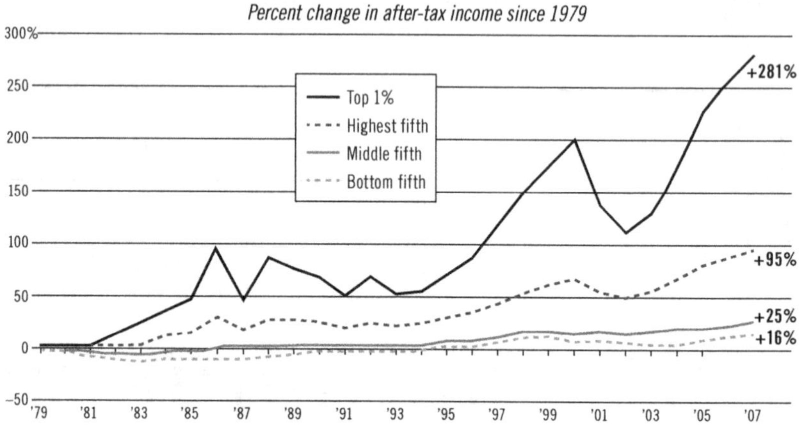
Percent change in after-tax income since 1979
300%
250
200
150
100
50
0
–50
'79
'81
'83
'85
'87
'89
'91
'93
'95
'97
'99
'01
'03
'05
'07
Top 1%
Highest fifth
Middle fifth
Bottom fifth
+281%
+95%
+25%
+16%

Source: CBPP calculations from Congressional Budget Office data.

Legal Apartheid

We are not only the global champs at income inequality, we are also the global leaders at locking up our own citizens. No nation has a higher rate of incarceration per capita than the United States. Our nation's census and justice data reveal a troubling, wildly accelerated climb in investment and response to investment in our systems of incarceration (see figure 2.5).[9]

According to *Mother Jones*'s "Debt to Society" project, which tracked prison investment and incarceration trends around the world from 1910–2000, between the early 1970s and 2000, the United States became the global leader on the project of incarcerating its citizens.[10] More recent research confirms that we have maintained our standing, with the world's highest total prison population (2,121,600) *and* incarceration rate per capita (655:100,000). For a point of comparison, China is second in total prison population, nearly half a million inmates behind us, and Russia is a distant third—nearly 1.5 mil-

FIGURE 2.5 Change in US incarceration rates, 1910–2000

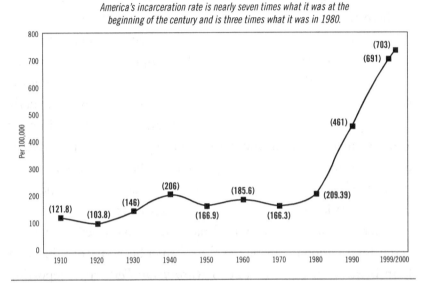

America's incarceration rate is nearly seven times what it was at the beginning of the century and is three times what it was in 1980.

Source: Justice Policy Institute analysis of Bureau of the Census and Bureau of Justice Statistics Data.

lion inmates behind us. In terms of per capita rates, El Salvador runs second, trailing the United States by over 6 percent (615:100,000). More notably, nation states like Cuba, Russia, and China, which we regularly criticize for their repressive state cultures, all have dramatically less commitment to their penal systems. Cuba's incarceration per capita (510:100,000) is 22 percent lower than ours, Russia's (375:100,000) is 43 percent lower, and China's (118:100,000) is a whopping 82 percent lower. So, while there are certainly ways in which the US culture provides freedoms that those other nation states do not, we are hardly the bastion of freedom and justice that would warrant us gallivanting around the world as a model to be emulated. It is no secret that our incarceration rates are also wildly disproportionate when disaggregated by race and income—yet another significant indictment against promises of an equal and meritocratic education system designed to be a "great equalizer."

In 1990, prison spending was one-sixteenth of our national school spending. Now it is one-eighth, a spending increase running at three times the rate of spending on education.[11] Why would a nation make such a radical and committed effort to expand its penal system if it actually believed in the prospect of a quality public education being the great equalizer for a democratic society? For the world of public education, the answer to this question is particularly troubling because what lies underneath these investment decisions is a commitment to a back-end investment in prisons in lieu of a front-end investment in schools. Simply put, in the national consciousness, the choice about the amount of public dollars to be spent on public education often pencils out as a "zero-sum game," the logic of which is rooted in deeply held racist and classist beliefs that undergird our national sensibilities.[12] As former Secretary of Education John B. King Jr. put it in a 2016 *Washington Post* article reporting on prison and school spending trends: "Budgets reflect our values, and the trends revealed in this analysis are a reflection of our nation's priorities that should be revisited. We need to invest more in prevention than in punishment, to invest more in schools, not prisons."[13]

These values and priorities to which King refers are not difficult to suss out if we look back at the history of the nation or, more recently, at the history of *Plessy* and *Brown* discussed in chapter 1. The truth is that we live in a racist and classist society where, deep down, many people believe that investing in children and families of color and those living in poverty is a wasted investment.[14] When that long-held sentiment is brought to bear on a zero-sum equation, then a front-end investment in education is social suicide because there will not be enough back-end money to insure the law-and-order infrastructure to deal with the lack of return on those failed education investments. So, while virtually every president since Andrew Johnson has made education a part of their political platform, the nation continues to hedge its bets more and more toward the back end in the communities in our society where we can least afford to have educational disinvestment.

WHEN AN EQUAL EDUCATION SYSTEM MOVES YOU FURTHER FROM PEACE AND PROSPERITY

In 2007, the Institute for Economics and Peace (IEP), in partnership with the Economist Intelligence Unit (EIU), launched the Global Peace Index (GPI), work they describe as a "data-led perspective on peace, security and development."[15] The IEP is now considered the world's leading think tank dedicated to developing metrics to analyze peace and to quantify its economic value. The IEP's research is regularly used by influential international groups such as the Organisation for Economic Cooperation and Development, the World Bank, and the United Nations. The GPI is like any index in that it is worthy of some debate. There are some items that maybe should not be included in the measurements, and there are probably some that could be added. Nevertheless, it is considered the global gold standard for measuring peace, security, and sustainable development in 163 nations and territories that cover 99.7 percent of the world's population. The GPI is widely accepted in research and policy circles as a reliable tool to show the statistical relationship between peacefulness and national wealth, and it has been enthusiastically endorsed by a host of notable global leaders, including former United Nations Secretary-General Kofi Annan, the Dalai Lama, Archbishop Desmond Tutu, former president of Finland and 2008 Nobel Peace Prize Laureate Martti Ahtisaari, Nobel Laureate Muhammad Yunus, former president of Ireland Mary Robinson, and former United States President Jimmy Carter.

When the index was first released, the United States was fifty-three years into its commitment to an equal education system. For a nation as obsessed with rankings as we have been, our initial placement at number 96, just below Yemen, might have been cause for alarm. If it was, there is nothing in the future rankings that suggests the alarm bells resulted in any notable course correction. Quite to the contrary, the US has been steadily sliding backward on the GPI, currently finding itself at 128, just below post-Apartheid South Africa.

I can certainly wrap my head around the argument that measuring things like peace, security, and development can be difficult and will likely always be an inexact science. But, if you are going to score well on any index, particularly as the self-proclaimed global referee of peace and democracy, you probably want to score well on something called the "Global Peace Index." The challenge presented by the GPI for so many of us doing work in the education sector is that virtually none of us currently live at 128. In fact, most of us probably live somewhere in the top thirty. So, what does that ranking mean for those children who are struggling the most in school right now if many of us are living considerably higher than our overall ranking? The simple math of it is probably best captured by a story I heard Bryan Stevenson share.

Stevenson is arguably the nation's most prominent death row lawyer and founder of the Equal Justice Initiative (EJI). In 2016, I attended an award ceremony hosted by the Black Googlers Network (BGN) at Google's main campus in Mountain View, California. The BGN's Racial Justice Fund was presenting an award to the Roses in Concrete Community School—an East Oakland school of which I am a founding member—along with two other organizations, one of which was the EJI. Stevenson keynoted the event and made a brilliant argument about the importance of proximity and remembering as antecedents to justice.[16] Stevenson's point about proximity is particularly important to consider as we think about what to make of where many of our children's experiences land them on the GPI.

His argument makes the salient point that while our nation has truly brilliant and committed people who are working tirelessly to improve the educational experiences of our children, they are designing their interventions without any real proximity to the pain that they are trying to resolve. In the absence of this proximity, solutions designed to relieve the pain of a life below 128 end up being no more than aspirin. And while aspirin may provide temporary relief for the symptoms of a headache, it does not stop one from getting headaches. The real solutions to the suffering and woundedness we are seeing in so many children must come from gaining real proximity to their pain and listening closely to solutions born out of the wisdom that comes from living through those experiences. The learning made possible by proximity must be our guide to remaking classrooms and schools so that the experiences our children receive there reflect a community-responsive pedagogy that relieves the suffering caused by our radically unequal society.[17] Only then will the data reflect trends that suggest we are heading toward a pluralistic, multiracial democracy committed to peace, prosperity, and sustainability.

THE PRINCIPAL FACTS: PLACE AND PROXIMITY TO PAIN MATTER

In addition to wanting to be data driven, I often hear schools and districts express the desire to be research based. I could get behind a commitment for our schools to be data driven and research based, so long as we take seriously what this tells us about where we are as a society and the changes it would demand in our schools. Were we to be so bold, we would do well to heed the following words from James Baldwin's essay "Nobody Knows my Name":

> What it comes to, finally, is that the nation has spent a large part
> of its time and energy looking away from one of the principal

facts of its life. This failure to look reality in the face diminishes a nation as it diminishes a person . . . Any honest examination of the national life proves how far we are from the standard of human freedom with which we began. The recovery of this standard demands of everyone who loves this country a hard look at [their self], for the greatest achievement must begin somewhere, and they always begin with the person. If we are not capable of this examination, we may yet become one of the most distinguished and monumental failures in the history of nations.[18]

Baldwin's essay offers a strategy for the nation to live up to its lofty ideals, one that demands the courage to confront the principal facts of our shortcomings and the creativity to correct them. Were we to engage such an endeavor, schools would need to play a significantly different role in our society, shifting from reinforcing the status quo to redefining it.

Any such discussion of creating schools that prepare young people to take on the seemingly intractable forms of inequity facing our society will require us to pay closer attention to the research on the social indicators of health. To this end, our examination of the data should explore the most cutting-edge, and also some of the most established, research in fields such as public health, physiology, community psychology, social epidemiology, neuroscience, and medicine. Without such a commitment, we will continually fail to address the needs of our most vulnerable children. But to adopt this approach would force a conversation guided by proximity and responsiveness to the "socially toxic environments" that emerge from racism, poverty, patriarchy, heterosexism, and all other forms of oppression.[19] Given the abysmal performance record of schools serving our nation's most wounded youth, it seems high time that those of us working to transform schools in the interest of that group of children heed Baldwin's advice and take a long look at ourselves. What we are doing is not working, and if we are honest, we will admit that it has never worked for the children who need us the most.

The aforementioned fields have increasingly turned their attention to identifying and understanding the social indicators of health and well-being. For education, this is the idea that "place"—the conditions in which children live—must be understood for schools to be effective.[20] This research reveals clearly identifiable social toxins that young people face in the broader society, and these are the "principal facts" for education to confront. By allowing our thinking and actions to be driven by the data emerging from this research, we are better positioned to treat our schools and classrooms as micro-ecosystems committed to "radical healing"[21] and "critical hope"[22] such that they are responsive to a meta-ecosystem that is wrought with inequity and social toxicity.[23]

Youth living at or below the GPI's 120s are growing up in areas that are entrenched in persistent cross-generational poverty—typically overrepresented by youth of color—where the rate of violence (physical and institutional) is high and legitimate living wage employment options are low. These youth frequently attend public schools that are under-resourced and have disturbingly low completion rates. David Williams of the Harvard School of Public Health argues that these conditions result in the "accumulation of multiple negative stressors, and it is so many of them [that it is] as if someone is being hit from every single side. And, it is not only that they are dealing with a lot of stress, [it is that] they have few resources to cope."[24] For decades, research has repeatedly shown that the accumulation of these negative social stressors acts as a real and persistent threat to hope for youth, inhibits academic performance and social development, and has serious long-term health implications.[25] The exposure to chronic stress associated with living in these types of socially toxic environments is now thought of as one of the most, if not *the* most, significant contributor to poor health and academic difficulties for children. By logical extension, a school's ability to respond to these "unnatural causes" of inequality will deeply impact educational outcomes for students.[26]

The implications of students' exposure to chronic stress for teaching and learning are profound. Consider Maslow's hierarchy of needs, which defined a person's primary human needs (food, clothing, shelter, safety) as prerequisites for pursuing needs higher up on the scale (such as education).[27] When we connect the dots between Maslow's framework and the latest research on unequal access to the social indicators of health, a serious dilemma is revealed for youth whose exposure to unremitting stressors leaves most (sometimes all) of their primary human needs under constant attack.[28]

According to Williams, "In our society today, everybody experiences stress. In fact, the person who has no stress is the person who is dead."[29] The body's stress response "calls forth the release of adrenaline and adrenocortical hormones" (such as cortisol), which have positive adaptive and protective functions for the body, including increased memory and muscle function.[30] Under normal conditions (see figure 2.6), the body's heightened response is maintained for an appropriate amount of time and then slowly recedes during a recovery period.

However, youth of color and youth living in poverty are often faced with repeated or unremitting stressors such that their bodies are denied the necessary recovery period (see figures 2.7 and 2.8).

Extensive research has reinforced findings that under these social conditions, the normally protective and adaptive function of the stress response is lost, as the overproduction of "stress mediators" are toxic to the body.[31] According to research in medicine and public health, these conditions produce an "allostatic load"—the

FIGURE 2.6 Normal stress response

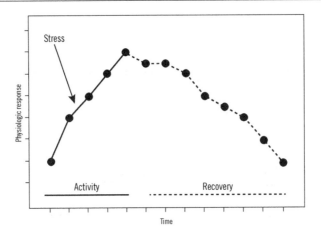

Source: Bruce S. McEwen and Teresa Seeman, "Protective and Damaging Effects of Mediators of Stress: Elaborating and Testing the Concepts of Allostasis and Allostatic Load," *Annals of the NY Academy of Science* 896, no. 1 (1999): 30–47, doi: 10.1111/j.1749-6632.1999.tb08103.x. PMID: 10681886.

FIGURE 2.7 Effect of repeated hits from "novel stressors"

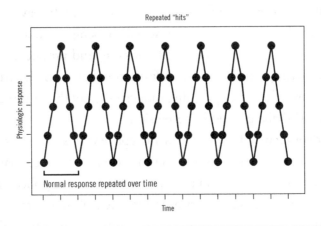

Source: Bruce S. McEwen and Teresa Seeman, "Protective and Damaging Effects of Mediators of Stress: Elaborating and Testing the Concepts of Allostasis and Allostatic Load," *Annals of the NY Academy of Science* 896, no. 1 (1999): 30–47, doi: 10.1111/j.1749-6632.1999.tb08103.x. PMID: 10681886.

FIGURE 2.8 Prolonged response due to delayed shutdown

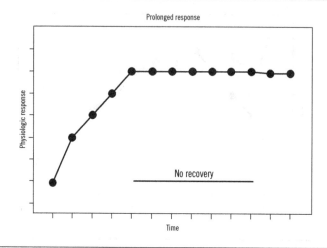

Source: Bruce S. McEwen and Teresa Seeman, "Protective and Damaging Effects of Mediators of Stress: Elaborating and Testing the Concepts of Allostasis and Allostatic Load," *Annals of the NY Academy of Science* 896, no. 1 (1999): 30–47, doi: 10.1111/j.1749-6632.1999.tb08103.x. PMID: 10681886.

"cumulative negative effects, or the price the body pays for being forced to adapt to various psychosocial challenges and adverse environments."[32] Over time, this load stacks up and produces the effect of "weathering" on the body.[33] Weathering has been shown to be a major cause of diseases plaguing modern society (heart disease, cancer, type II diabetes, and hypertension).[34]

For young people whose lives are replete with social stressors over which they feel little control (racism, poverty, violence, patriarchy, heterosexism, environmental toxins, gentrification, police brutality, xenophobia, language discrimination, lack of access to nutrition, substandard education, substandard housing, substandard health care), their systems are forced to work overtime, all the time. These are our most wounded children and therefore the ones whom our public school systems should be the most responsible for serving.[35]

An expansive and growing body of research in the fields of health, social epidemiology, psychology, and social science describes four major sources of traumatic stress that educators must be prepared to address as leading causes of wounded children: (1) institutional violence; (2) physical violence; (3) root shock; and (4) wealth inequality.

Institutional Violence

When we think about the ways that violence impacts youth, it is important to understand that violence operates through institutional norms as well as through interpersonal physical conflict. The list of forms of institutional violence is too long to be comprehensively covered here. Instead, I will highlight some of the most pernicious and pervasive forms of institutional violence to which educators should be prepared to respond.

In efforts to understand institutional violence, "one should not look for the gross and obvious."[36] Rather, institutional violence tends to take the shape of *microaggressions*, defined as "subtle insults (verbal, nonverbal, and/or visual) . . . [that occur] often automatically or unconsciously.[37] In isolation, these events may seem harmless, but their cumulative impact is debilitating and numerous studies identify them as leading causes of persistent social stress.[38] Research here is conclusive. In each area that someone's identity falls outside of the dominant cultural norms of this country (white, heterosexual, male, English-speaking, middle-class, able-bodied), they will experience forms of institutional violence. The further one's identity is from this norm, the greater the potential that their institutional experiences will result in the accumulation of multiple negative social stressors.

Three specific terms are worth noting here as important additions to the educational lexicon on institutional violence: poverty tax, eco-apartheid, and infra-racial racism. *Poverty tax* is a term describing the hidden tax poor communities pay as a result of limited options for virtually every essential service (banking, groceries, health care,

housing, transportation).[39] *Eco-apartheid* describes the disproportionate stacking of ecologically toxic conditions in poor communities of color.[40] Extending Van Jones's original definition,[41] Akom
describes eco-apartheid as:

> . . . the ways in which historical legacies, individuals, structures,
> and institutions work together to distribute material and sym-
> bolic advantages and disadvantages along racial lines (Powell,
> 2008). At the macro level, eco-apartheid helps us analyze how
> health, housing, education, transportation, and other systems
> "interact across domains and over time to produce unintended
> consequences with clear racialized effects" (Powell, 2008, p. 791).
> Such an approach allows researchers to move beyond individu-
> alized understandings of "meritocracy" to demonstrate the ways
> in which all groups are interconnected and how structures shape
> command over resources and life chances (Akom, 2008). At the
> level of cultural understanding, eco-apartheid shows how the
> structures we create, develop, and maintain in turn impact our
> racial and social identities by shaping the production of knowl-
> edge and naturalizing social meanings.[42]

Finally, *infra-racial racism* describes "the actual mental, physical, epistemological, and ontological harm, beyond the visible end
of the spectrum, that racism does to Black people/people of color in
everyday life; as well as accounting for how cumulative advantages
are gained by whites and lighter skinned people."[43]

Each of these ideas narrates institutional violence in a way that
helps us understand it as a phenomenon that has a cumulative impact over time, threatening essential forms of institutional security:
citizenship, jobs, schools, neighborhoods, hospitals, health care, and
legal outcomes.[44]

Physical Violence

The fact that witnessing or experiencing physical violence contributes to a person's traumatic stress load is common sense. What is not often clear to educators is the frequency and intensity with which this happens to youth, and the medical research that suggests this may be one of the biggest inhibitors to academic success.[45] The national data set on youth trauma suggests that as many as one-third of children living in urban poverty show symptoms of post-traumatic stress disorder (PTSD), a rate nearly twice that found in soldiers returning from live combat.[46] Complexifying the issue is the fact that while soldiers leave the battlefield, young people do not. This suggests that for youth who are repeatedly exposed to violent traumatic events, modifiers like "perpetual" or "persistent" would more accurately describe their experiences than the commonly used "post" traumatic stress.

Public health research has identified physical violence as one the biggest threats to well-being among children. According to Robert Prentice, senior associate for Public Health Policy and Practice at the Public Health Institute (CA), "the specter of community violence has completely transformed the way people live in certain neighborhoods. So, it's a public health issue not only for the prevention of early death through homicide, but for the ripple effects it has on the other things that contribute to people's poor health—the ability to go out, to go shopping, to live a normal life."[47]

Jack Shonkoff, a pediatrician at Harvard's Center on the Developing Child, argues that studies indicate that exposure to violence "triggers physiological responses in a child and can actually be disruptive to the developing brain and immune system such that you are primed to be more vulnerable to physical and mental health problems throughout your life."[48] These concerns are echoed by findings from Stanford University's Early Life Stress Research Program.[49] The program's director, Victor Carrion, argues that PTSD "feeds on avoidance. The more you avoid it, the worse it gets."[50] His belief that schools have an important role to play in healing this trauma in youth has led him to begin trainings with urban schools to help educators identify the symptoms of PTSD so they can get their students access to treatment.

Root Shock

Root shock is a metaphor borrowed from botany to describe "the traumatic stress reaction to the destruction of all or part of one's emotional ecosystem."[51] Plants suffer from root shock when they are relocated. The loss of familiar soil and its balanced nutrients is damaging to the root system. The term was coined by Fullilove to describe the impact of gentrification projects (often referred to as "urban renewal") that create neighborhood displacement. Other studies have shown the harmful impacts of being ripped from roots by analyzing groups, particularly Indigenous groups exposed to colonialism, who have suffered losses of language, land, and/or culture.[52] Educators must understand the impact of historical cultural genocide, ongoing cultural disenfranchisement, and recent thrusts of urban gentrification projects on their students so they can develop pedagogical responses and avoid contributing to those conditions.

Wealth Inequality

Although I am convinced that wealth inequality is a form of structural violence, I have separated it out for the purposes of distinguishing it from traditional notions of poverty. According to health researchers, the unremitting stress of childhood poverty produces a daily toxic burden from not knowing whether they will have a roof over their heads, food on the table, electricity, heat, or clean water.[53] Shonkoff describes this effect as a "pile up of risk: the cumulative burden of things that increase your chances of having problems, as opposed to the cumulative protection of having things in your life that increase the likelihood that you are going to have better outcomes."[54]

However, poverty alone does not explain the fact that at the turn of the century, the World Health Organization ranked the United States dead last in health outcomes among the world's industrialized nations, despite spending $2 trillion on health care per year (nearly half the health dollars spent globally).[55] "The position of the United States was one of the major surprises of the new rating system. Basically, you die earlier and spend more time disabled if you're an American rather than a member of most other advanced countries," says Christopher Murray, former Director of WHO's Global Programme on Evidence for Health Policy.[56] In the WHO's press release about the report, Murray's primary explanation for these seemingly inexplicable results centered radicalized race and class inequalities: "In the United States, some groups, such as Native Americans, rural African Americans and the inner city poor, have extremely poor health, more characteristic of a poor developing country rather than a rich industrialized one."[57]

Health research on the impact of these conditions of poverty suggests that the negative effects are exacerbated when they occur in the face of great wealth. Despite wealth inequality reaching record lows in 1976, the United States is now "far and away the most unequal of the world's rich democracies" and getting worse.[58] To be entrenched in intergenerational poverty in a country where wealth is flaunted and constantly visible and the rhetoric of meritocracy reigns supreme, adds an additional layer of stress by intensifying awareness of one's own poverty. Akom describes this as a by-product of "Ameritocracy," a largely US phenomenon where the nation preserves the rhetoric of meritocracy despite a reality that presents us with overwhelming evidence of stark inequality and unearned privilege.[59] In this sense, wealth inequality is different from poverty because wealth inequality accounts for the additional stress experienced by youth who are constantly made aware of all the things they do not have in their lives as result of their poverty.

CUT OFF THE HANDLE

In August of 1854, there was a massive outbreak of cholera in the Soho section of London. In less than two weeks, five hundred people had died and nearly three-quarters of the residents had fled the area. The prevailing logic in the medical community at the time, which was known as the Miasma Theory, was that cholera was airborne and passed through "bad air, arising from decayed organic matter or miasmata."[60] One young doctor, John Snow, went against that prevailing logic, arguing that cholera was a germ pathogen that was spread through water. Leading medical officials in the city such as Dr. John Simon, who was the head medical officer in the city at the time, called Snow's theory "peculiar," in part because the actual germ that causes cholera would not be officially discovered until some twenty-five years after Snow's death.

Despite the blowback from the medical community, Snow was convinced that cholera was being passed through drinking water. To prove his theory, Snow became an ethnographer of the community he was serving. He got proximity. He started collecting data. Snow interviewed as many people as he could who had cholera and as many people as he could who did not. What he found in his data is a researcher's dream. He found causality. When Snow plotted incidences of cholera around water pumps, the dot map he created clearly illustrated that one particular pump, the Broad Street Pump, was the source of the outbreak. Everyone Snow interviewed who contracted cholera during that outbreak drank from that water fountain and everyone who did not contract cholera didn't. Snow convinced city officials to cut off the handle to the pump, and the wave of cholera stopped.

How much more data do we need before we cut off the handle to the poisoned well of an equal education system in a radically unequal society? The research and copious data presented throughout this chapter suggest that we are hurtling at breakneck speed toward a cliff, the edge of which is the social and political death of our democracy. Any attempts to duck, dodge, or deny that reality only hastens that death. We are past the point where we can just continue to huddle around a policy table and wring our hands; we have to act now, we have to act decisively, and we have to act with an urgency that reflects an understanding that we are staring down the barrel of a measurable existential threat to our national existence that is the social equivalent of the climate catastrophe that also sits on our immediate horizon. There is simply nothing in our national data that suggests that the path we are on has the potential to produce the pluralistic multiracial democracy we have promised to our children. We will significantly change or we will perish. It's that serious.

PUBLIC SCHOOLS FOR WHAT? MEASURING WHAT MATTERS TO MAKE SURE IT NEVER HAPPENS AGAIN

The pivot toward an equitable education system begins with us asking and genuinely wrestling with the question of *why* we even have public schools in the first place. Why do we take children away from their families at the age of five, for thirteen consecutive years, for seven hours a day? If our aim is to create a radically unequal and undemocratic society—replete with widespread civic disengagement and disenfranchisement, rates of poor health and violence that rival the world's most unstable societies, and perpetual denial of a deeply imbedded cultural legacy of white supremacy, colonialism, and genocide—then let us be calm and carry on.

If, however, we aim to bring up a generation of children who mature into healthy, engaged, critical civic participants who are actually prepared to meet the challenges laid out before us in this chapter, then we'd best get to the work of remembering. On that point of remembering, I return to Bryan Stevenson's work. His theory of change demands pairing remembering with the aforementioned perspective gained through proximity to pain. For Stevenson, the only way to make sure that the travesties of our past do not happen again is to make sure that no one ever forgets that they happened. In his writing and his speaking, Stevenson frequently cites three international examples of nations that committed to "changing their narrative" by remembering.

In 1994, nearly 800,000 people in Rwanda were slaughtered in one hundred days in an atrocious genocide. To begin the long road back from this horrific event, Rwanda committed itself to telling the truth about the genocide in every corner of its society. According to Stevenson, "You cannot spend a day in Rwanda without the people talking to you about the genocide. It's urgent to them that everyone understand what happened there."[61]

When apartheid ended in South Africa, there was acknowledgment that the country would need to commit to a process of truth and reconciliation. The Truth and Reconciliation Commission was established where victims of extreme human rights violations were invited to give testimonials about their suffering, and some of these testimonials became parts of public hearings. The Constitutional Court in Johannesburg is replete with images, language, and iconography reminding all that go there of the brutality and lasting impact of apartheid.

In Germany, Stevenson remarks:

You cannot go 200 meters without seeing the markers, or monuments, or stones that have been placed next to the homes of Jewish families that were abducted during the Holocaust. The Germans actually want you to go to the Holocaust Memorial . . .

There are no Adolf Hitler statues in Germany. Swastikas have been banned. There's a consciousness to never again fall prey to the politics of fear and anger that gave rise to that Holocaust. In this country we don't talk about slavery, we don't talk about Native genocide, we don't talk about lynching, we don't talk about segregation. You start talking about race and people get nervous. You start talking about racial justice and people are looking for exits. Our landscape is littered with iconography designed to romanticize the period of enslavement, to celebrate and honor the architects of slavery.[62]

The US State Department is funded to assist in transitional justice efforts such as these around the world, but we have never committed to this sort of truth and reconciliation for our own country. For Stevenson, "until we understand the truth of our history, every effort at repair will fail."[63] Our nation is infected with the legacy of white supremacy and radicalized inequality. It is our national disease. We have to treat it.

I want to encourage the growing interest among schools and districts to be data driven. We must be data driven, but the data that we are collecting and using to drive funding, policy, and practice must measure what really matters in the pursuit of freedom, justice, and democracy. This means reorienting the primary purpose of our public school system to one that is committed to generational health above generational wealth, developing young people who love themselves and all the people of this planet enough to never allow us to forget how we got into this mess, so that we can get out of this mess, so that we never end up in this mess again.

CHAPTER 3

EQUITY IS THE SUPERIOR GROWTH MODEL

> Turning and turning in the widening gyre
> The falcon cannot hear the falconer;
> Things fall apart; the centre cannot hold;
> Mere anarchy is loosed upon the world,
> The blood-dimmed tide is loosed, and everywhere
> The ceremony of innocence is drowned;
> The best lack all conviction, while the worst
> Are full of passionate intensity.
>
> —William Butler Yeats, "The Second Coming"

In 2011, PolicyLink released a report in collaboration with the University of Southern California's Program for Environmental and Regional Equity (PERE) entitled "America's Tomorrow: Equity is the Superior Growth Model."[1] The report concludes that consistent and persistent investments in policies and practices that promote equity show the best prospects for continued and sustainable growth for the nation. Frankly, there is no real debate in the research community about whether equity is the way to go for countries looking to achieve happiness and wellness for their citizenry and longevity for their society. Danny Dorling, a social geographer, and Halford Mackinder, professor of geography at the University of Oxford, argue that the effect of a more equitable society "can appear magical. . . . human beings are generally happier and healthier; there is less crime, more creativity, more productivity, and—overall—higher real educational attainment. The evidence for the benefits of living more economically equitable lives is now so overwhelming that it will soon start to change politics and societies all over the world."[2]

As chapters 1 and 2 have clearly laid out, the body of research on the necessity for social and economic equity is immense, it is growing, and it is conclusive. The core conditions that would create more widespread social prosperity are consistently illuminated in this research. They are not mysterious to us, nor is the significant role that public education must play in the establishment, growth, and maintenance of these conditions in a society. Indeed, schools are the institution that is best positioned to prepare a nation's youth to build and maintain an equitable society.

When we cross-reference the decades of research on equitable teacher and school practices, the consistency of findings from those studies is striking. Year after year and study after study, the conclusions remain pretty much the same; which is to say that the framework for classrooms and schools to be on the path to equity is bounded by three domains for teaching and school culture: relationships, relevance, and responsibility. These domains, along with ways to achieve and measure them, are the focus of the next four chapters of this book.

EQUITY? SURE. BUT FOR WHAT?

In an equitable system, if you are hungry, you get food. If you are thirsty, you get water. In an equitable education system, young people get what they need *when* they need it. This is not a new idea. Instructionally, we have considered this the gold standard for effective pedagogy for decades (if not centuries) in the form of differentiated instruction. But the skill and will that it takes to actually deliver on the promise of an equitable education system require a kind of investment in our education system that this nation has been loath to make. The result is what Langston Hughes refers to as the "dream deferred":

What happens to a dream deferred?

Does it dry up
Like a raisin in the sun?

Or fester like a sore—
And then run?

Does it stink like rotten meat?
Or crust and sugar over—
like a syrupy sweet?

Maybe it just sags
like a heavy load.

Or does it explode?[3]

For children all over this nation, particularly those relentlessly forced to bear the unearned burden of poverty or white supremacy (or both), each of Hughes's stanzas is likely true at different moments in their time in our nation's public education system. The consistent deferring of the dreams of our nation's most vulnerable youth in our schools is not the result of not knowing that this is happening. It is not the result of not knowing how to inspire and support the dreams of children. Rather, it is the outcome of what Martin Luther King, Jr., calls the "tranquilizing drug of gradualism"[4]—a historical hyper-investment in the rhetoric of meritocracy, which ultimately plays itself out as a seemingly never-ending process of hand-wringing and intellectual self-flagellation about the importance of doing better for "all" children without ever stating *when* we will commit to doing things completely differently with the children who need things to be completely different. To make that sort of commitment would require us to admit that the public school system we have created is designed to fail those who need it the most. This admission of guilt—and we *are* guilty of having perpetuated a system that was designed to build exactly the kind of social and economic apartheid that is tearing at the very fabric of our democracy—would demand that we rethink the very purpose of public education in our society. In so doing, we would be staring at perhaps the three most important questions we must continually interrogate to pursue an equitable education system: (1) Equity for what? (2) Equity how? and (3) Equity when?

EQUITY—FOR WHAT?

Of these three questions, the answer to the first is the simplest and easily located in the troubling and persistently tragic data produced by our decades of systemic inequality. The primary purpose of a national public education system should be the development of the well-being of our children, for the well-being of our communities, for the well-being of our society, for the well-being of our planet. Simply put, children should leave school more well in their mind, body, and spirit than when they came, and they should understand the connectedness and responsibility to uphold this wellness in our society and planet for future generations. Every aspect of our schools should reflect this commitment: curriculum, pedagogy, school and classroom climates, physical plant (buildings and grounds), nutrition, design of the school day, and assessment.

If we were to be so committed, our schools and classrooms would prioritize an awareness of Maslow's statement that "the basic human needs are organized into a hierarchy of relative prepotency."[5] His paper entitled "A Theory of Human Motivation," released in 1943, led to the development of the hierarchy of needs, a framework for well-being that has since been continually reified, study after study, across a wide range of fields. Simply put, there is nothing being used in US schools that has the research base of Maslow. Nothing even comes close.

But Maslow's framework has a historical origin that demands our understanding if we are to properly operationalize it. A number of Indigenous scholars have made the case that Maslow developed his theory of human needs while riding on the wings of Indigenous thought. Cindy Blackstock (a member of the Gitxsan tribe (executive director of the First Nations Child and Family Caring Society of Canada and professor for the School of Social Work at McGill University) and Leroy Little Bear (a member of the Blackfoot tribe, professor emeritus at the University of Lethbridge, and founding member of Canada's first Native American Studies department) are arguably the most prominent of these voices. In 2004, however, Indigenous researchers Ryan Heavy Head and Narcisse Blood engaged in the most thorough investigation of the influence of Indigenous knowledge about human wellness on Maslow's work. Their three-year study, the presentation for which is entitled "Naamitapiikoan: Blackfoot Influences on Abraham Maslow's Developmental and Organizational Psychology" provides incredible insight into the profound and mostly unacknowledged influence that the Blackfoot people had on Maslow's now-famous paper and hierarchy of needs framework.[6]

The biographical research conducted by Heavy Head and Blood reveals that in the mid-1930s, Maslow was a newly minted PhD and crafting a research paradigm to support his belief that the human species had identifiable, consistent developmental patterns that governed social development, norms, and practices. He brought this belief to a colloquium in New York City that was convened by Ruth Benedict, a well-regarded anthropologist of that period. Maslow shared with the group that he was working on a paradigm that supported his theory that the "universal human experience was that of a social hierarchy that was developed through displays of aggression."[7] Benedict challenged Maslow to test his theory outside of his immediate, culturally constrained, Western, male, and white worldview. Benedict created the opportunity for Maslow to test his theory with the Blackfoot people on the reserve known as Siksika through her connections to research being done with Indigenous tribes in Canada.[8]

Maslow showed up at Siksika, near Alberta, Canada, in the summer of 1938. His six weeks among the Blackfoot people profoundly influenced his theory of "innate positivity in human beings and pointed towards a more benevolent form of society."[9] According to Maslow's biographer Edward Hoffman, upon his return to New York from Siksika, Maslow was immediately "conceptualizing a new biologically rooted but humanistic approach to personality transcending the narrowness of cultural relativism."[10]

The evidence of the influence of Indigenous thought on Maslow's framework abounds, but what might be most striking and important for the purposes of this discussion are the ways he bent the teachings he received to fit a Western, white, patriarchal, and colonialist model of well-being. The framework Maslow developed stops where Indigenous paradigms of wellness begin. The individual self-actualization that Maslow places at the pinnacle of his hierarchy may indeed be consistently possible only when the other tiers (physiological, safety, love and belonging, and esteem) are consistently realized. So, in a society that is so profoundly unequal and inequitable, Maslow's framework may need to be our guide to do for children what any civilized society should already be doing if it had the resources that we have as a nation.

The primary purpose of *every* school should be to cultivate the well-being of *every* child, and Maslow's hierarchy of needs provides a solid framework to that end. So, yes, perhaps we actually need to say that we intend to make those investments in every child, no matter the cost, since at the moment, that seems to be a promise made only to some—and mostly white, middle-class/wealthy, English-speaking, heterosexual, male—children. The Blackfoot teachings that Maslow was gifted seem to have taught him the absolute value of those commitments for the development of a caring, connected, and truly democratic community. But the question for Maslow is the same question facing public schools—for what? The answer to that question in both instances is the same, and it is the essence of the Blackfoot teachings that Maslow either missed or ignored.

The First Nations perspective (see figure 3.1 below) that so profoundly influenced Maslow treats self-actualization as the beginning of an individual's journey.[11] In this perspective, one self-actualizes to contribute to community actualization, and the community actualizes for cultural perpetuity, ensuring the passing along of the wisdom of past achievements and failures. There is no room there for a historical amnesia that erases past mistakes. One self-actualizes so that the community can constantly learn, grow, adapt, and improve, carrying forward the essence of one's ancestral cultures and applying the hard lessons of the past by modeling truth telling and reconciliation with one's children.

The aim of public schools should be the development of children's natural ability to self-actualize. Schools should prioritize the physiological, safety, love and belonging, and esteem needs of all

FIGURE 3.1 Maslow's Hierarchy of needs, informed by the Blackfoot nation

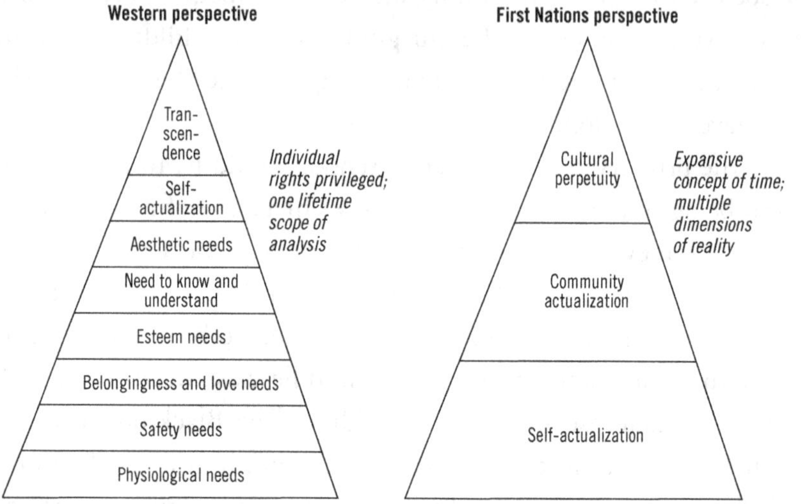

Western perspective

Tran-
scen-
dence

Self-
actualization

Aesthetic needs

Need to know and
understand

Esteem needs

Belongingness and love needs

Safety needs

Physiological needs

*Individual
rights privileged;
one lifetime
scope of
analysis*

First Nations perspective

Cultural
perpetuity

Community
actualization

Self-actualization

*Expansive
concept of time;
multiple
dimensions
of reality*

Source: Cindy Blackstock, "When Everything Matters: What Happens to Children When They Are Brought into Care?" lecture delivered at the 32nd Annual National Indian Child Welfare Association Conference, Fort Lauderdale, FL, 2014.

children, and they should do so in a way that is culturally mediated—precisely as Maslow suggested. But Maslow, like our schools, lost track of the purpose of self-actualization in a healthy democratic society. Maslow's framework as a pathway to wellness is wholly individualistic, just like almost every way that we talk about measurable achievement in schools.

We have designed public schools with a purpose. That purposeful design will forever give us exactly what we are currently getting out of schools. If we reverse engineer this equation, then we can conclude that to change outcomes, we must meaningfully change the design; and to change design in that manner, we must change the purpose of public schools.

This idea of appropriating and then bastardizing Indigenous ways of being, knowing, and governing to suit our nation's Eurocentric worldview is not unique to Maslow. Both Thomas Jefferson and Benjamin Franklin were "influenced by the Iroquois model of democratic government, with its system of checks and balances and elected representatives."[12] It is well established that our constitution, and our democracy as we know it, were attempts to deploy a system similar to what early colonizers saw in the Haudenosaunee (Six Nations Iroquois Confederacy), which is described in the "Haudenosaunee Statement to the World" as being "among the most ancient continuously operating governments in the world. Long before the arrival of the European peoples in North America, our people met in council to enact the principles of peaceful coexistence among nations and in recognition of the right of peoples to continue an uninterrupted existence."[13]

As a matter of national course correction, we should go back to those places of great wisdom that the "founding fathers" and Maslow found so valuable all those years ago. But this time around, let us go humbly, seeking the guidance to remake our public school system in a way that reflects a national purpose of growing and sustaining the well-being of our children in service of a just and sustainable democracy.

EQUITY—HOW?

Were we to choose equity as our model and the well-being of children as our purpose, we could draw from a plethora of research and evidence-based strategies to rebuild schools to meet this challenge to change. Over the past sixty years, numerous studies have supported the importance of Maslow's framework for individual well-being. A similarly voluminous set of studies has consistently identified the following three pedagogical domains (relationships, relevance, and responsibility) as foundational for building classroom cultures and climates that cultivate and sustain individual well-being development in children through intraconnectedness to self and interconnectedness to family, community, ancestors, and the natural world.

Relationships

The relationships domain consists of qualities of community-responsive schools and educators that are committed to building meaningful, caring relationships with students and families, guided by the understanding that children do not care what we know until they know that we care.[14] These relationships are the foundation for teachers, students, and families to create solidarity with and among each other. The connectedness that comes from that solidarity is essential for children to feel loved, and love is the fertile soil for durable and sustainable growth and development of children.[15] These types of relationships begin with daily acknowledgment and centering of the ancestral and community cultural wealth that students and families bring with them to school.[16] They promote an intraconnectedness for children that addresses the bottom four tiers of Maslow's hierarchy of needs (refer back to figure 3.1). They also intentionally develop interconnected relationships where all students, especially those who are most wounded and vulnerable, feel valued and part of something bigger than themselves.

Relevance

The relevance domain consists of qualities of community-responsive schools and educators that are committed to developing curriculum and pedagogy that center students' daily lives, their communities, their families, and their ethnic, cultural, and linguistic histories.[17] This connection must avoid the trap of multiculturalism and the reduction of culture to "trivial examples and artifacts of cultures such as eating ethnic or cultural foods, singing or dancing, reading folktales, and other less than scholarly pursuits of the fundamentally different conceptions of knowledge or quests for social justice."[18] A relevant pedagogy rigorously tunes instructional climate and curriculum to work across whatever tiers of Maslow's hierarchy a child might need on any given day. Via the centering of students, their families, their communities, and their ancestors, a relevant pedagogy acknowledges their histories and stories as assets that provide cultural wisdom and pathways to freedom and justice. This advances Maslow's individualistic frame toward one that allows children to use their learning to develop a sense of co-centric circles of interconnectedness (peers, school community, local community, larger society, and the natural world).

Responsibility

The responsibility domain consists of qualities of schools and educators that are committed to understanding and responding to the wide range of needs (social, emotional, spiritual, physical, and technical) that impact a student's capacity to be at their best. This responsiveness keeps in mind that attentiveness to the well-being of the child is simultaneously about the individual child *and* the wellness of the community, again returning Maslow's individualistic framework to its Blackfoot origins where meeting the needs of the individual child are connected to the larger purpose of community actualization. The community-responsive educator can hold these two otherwise distinct goals in the same developmental space as they consider their curriculum and pedagogical interventions. They can do this because they do not consider individual achievement as separate from community achievement. An individual child cannot be succeeding if the child next to them is failing. All boats must rise because it is all of us or none of us, and the classroom and school should be built accordingly. In these educational spaces, it is understood that hurt people tend to hurt people and people who are well tend to heal people. So, the wounds of an individual child are treated as the wounds of the entire classroom and school community because this fact is inescapable if we are truly interconnected (the rash of school shootings this nation has been experiencing is a painful reminder of this fact). Ergo, healing a child's wounds heals the classroom, school, and community entire.

All this to say that the responsibility domain reflects an approach to education that treats the classroom space as a micro-ecosystem of the micro-ecosystem of the school, both of which reflect the ecosystems of the community and the broader society. The forces of each layer of these social ecosystems impinge on one another in both directions; smaller systems pushing out to alter the larger systems and the larger systems pushing back and impacting the smaller ecosystems. This interconnectedness shows up every day in every school and every classroom. It requires schools and individual educators to find effective ways to identify what children need, when they need it, and to keep track of the degree to which those needs are being met. Meeting this responsibility requires schools and educators to acknowledge and leverage student strengths to develop and maintain their well-being and overall achievement.

EQUITY—WHEN?

I'd like to end this chapter by quoting from three people whose lives changed the world and set off sparks in the minds of others to try to do the same. The first of these mentors is El-Hajj Malik El-Shabazz, better known as Malcolm X, whose concluding remarks at the prestigious Oxford Union Debate in 1964 I will quote at length here, because I cannot think of a more profound way to describe the challenge in front of our field:

I believe that when a human being is exercising extremism in defense of liberty for human beings, it's no vice. And when one is moderate in pursuit of justice for human beings, he is a sinner. . . . I read once about a man named Shakespeare . . . He put it in the mouth of Hamlet . . . Whether it was nobler in the mind of man to suffer the slings and arrows of outrageous fortune— moderation. Or, to take up arms against a sea of troubles and by opposing, end them. I go for that. If you take up arms, you will end it. But, if you sit around and wait for the one who is in power to make up his mind that he should end it, you will be waiting a long time.

In my opinion, the young generation of whites, blacks, browns . . . you are living in a time of extremism, a time of revolution, a time when there has got to be a change. People in power have misused it and now there has to be a change and a better world has to be built and the only way it is going to be built is with extreme methods. I, for one, will join in with anyone. I do not care what color you are, as long as you want to change this miserable condition that exists on this earth.[19]

For those considering moderation, the alternative to El-Shabazz's preference, I would remind you of the example set for us by Harriet Tubman, who said in response to detractors of the "extreme" methods for which she advocated by freeing herself and leading the underground railroad: "I had reasoned this out in my mind; there was one of two things I had a right to, liberty, or death; if I could not have one, I would have the other; for no man should take me alive; I should fight for my liberty as long as my strength lasted, and when the time came for me to go, the Lord would let them take me."[20]

Our field can reach the level of commitment to human dignity put forth by these two ancestors by developing and supporting schools that meet Camangian's expectation that we "teach like our lives depend on it."[21] When we do, we spark minds that change the world. To be sure, the task presented by the research and data in front of us is monumental and growing—in short, we are facing a crisis state. Ironically, perhaps, the Educational Testing Service says that we face a "'perfect storm' of demographic, labor market, and educational trends that threatens the American dream."[22] Our willingness to be honest about the gravity of our situation is the first step out of this hole, but we must not twist this examination to create justifications for poor teaching and rationales for student failure. Quite the contrary: an examination of the array of inequalities facing vulnerable communities suggests that we should be all the more inspired as educators, knowing that we are working with young people whom Tupac Shakur referred to as the "roses that grow from concrete."[23] They are the ones who prove society's rule wrong by keeping the dream of a better society alive, growing in spite of the cold, uncaring, un-nurturing environment of the concrete. According to Shakur, educators should not "ask why the rose that [grows] from concrete [has] damaged petals. On the contrary, we [should] all celebrate its tenacity. We [should] all love its will to reach the sun."[24]

We must be openly critical of efforts that deny the tenacity and capacity of vulnerable youth and families, distorting truthful discussions of unequal social conditions in order to support models of cultural deficiency.[25] We must be honest about: (1) the complicity of dominant institutional forces in the disproportionate displacement of inequality onto poor and BIPOC communities; (2) the incredible resilience and capacity of individuals and communities that persist despite these inequalities; and (3) the ways in which individuals from all communities can be complicit in the maintenance of an unequal social order.

Simply put, people who ascribe to deficit models, blaming students and families for unequal social conditions, should not be permitted to work with vulnerable communities. In my experience and research, educators with these sensibilities and belief systems are present in our schools and our educational pipeline programs.[26] But they are rare. The majority of educators and aspiring educators I come across feel overwhelmed by the challenges youth face in their lives and consider themselves ill-equipped to respond with a pedagogy that will develop hope in the face of such daunting hardships. They are liberal-minded enough to avoid "blaming the victim," turning instead to blaming the "system" (the economy, the violence in society, the lack of social services). These educators have a critique of social inequality, but struggle to manifest this critique in any kind of transformative pedagogical project. They "hope" for change in its most deferred forms: either a collective utopia of a future reformed society or, more often, the individual student's future ascension to the middle class.[27]

Eventually, many students come to perceive a significant gap between their most pressing needs and the things being emphasized in the schooling we offer them (test scores, grades, college). When they figure out that schools are unwilling and/or unable to close this gap, their hope that school will be relevant in the context of their everyday lives is deferred. And, just as Martin Luther King, Jr., foretold of justice, hope too long deferred is hope denied.

The data on the well-being of this nation clearly suggests we have spun ourselves out wider and wider in a gyre of commitments destined to hurtle us toward a tipping point. We are on the brink of the society Yeats portends when the falcon (our children) can no longer hear the falconer (the promise of public schools) and the center (the prospect of an equal and just pluralistic, multiracial democracy) can no longer hold. We simply cannot afford to give over another generation of our children to a system that was never designed to build a healthy and sustainable democratic nation.

The good news is that we do not have to do it this way any longer. There is another way and it is better for all us, precisely because it is better for our children.

CHAPTER 4

RELATIONSHIPS

Children Don't Care What We Know
Until They Know That We Care

"Love recognizes no barriers. It jumps hurdles, leaps fences,
penetrates walls to arrive at its destination full of hope."

—Maya Angelou

If you have taught, you know that at the end of the day, teaching
and learning always boil down to one thing—relationships. Despite our widespread and constant investment in curriculum as the
antidote for poor engagement and achievement, there is simply no
evidence to suggest that curriculum will save us. You can have the
dopest curriculum ever known to humanity, but if you do not have
strong relationships, then children will blow it up. On the flip side,
you can have the wackest curriculum ever, and if you have strong relationships, the children will tolerate you long enough for you to get
your act together. For decades, researchers have sought to identify
things that matter most for effective teaching. Across both time and
place, study after study has concluded that all successful roads are

paved with caring relationships.[1] It is not that other things do not matter. Of course, curriculum, assessment, structure, resources and a host of other factors matter. But each of these other factors either impinge on or support the connected and caring relationships that sit in the divide between the unlimited potential of our children and how they actually perform in our schools.

WILLED NOT-LEARNING

Herb Kohl is one of the first US scholars to use an asset-based lens to examine the experiences of children whom school systems saw as failing. Where schools saw failure, Kohl saw "creative maladjustment." He was particularly intrigued by students who would consistently show up to school and put forth little to no effort to invest in behaviors that would manifest in their school success. He called this behavior "willed not-learning."[2] If you have been a teacher, particularly in schools that serve our most wounded youth, then you have surely experienced the phenomenon of having a child show up virtually every day of a marking period and then, when you review your gradebook to submit your grades, you are reminded that this child has turned nothing in—straight zeros across the gradebook. Kohl might well refer to this child as our most committed student. Think about the discipline that it takes to show up every single day and not turn in a single piece of work—*this* is willed not-learning. Or, as Kohl puts it, willed not-learning "consists of a conscious and chosen refusal to assent to learn. It manifests itself most often in withdrawal or defiance and is not just a school-related phenomenon."[3] Willed not-learning "is often and disastrously mistaken for failure to learn or the inability to learn."[4]

This approach to school may feel foreign to some, particularly those who came to school with childhood experiences that taught them that adults in power and mainstream social institutions could be trusted. But all of us understand the practice of willed not-learning—and probably better than we care to admit—because we all do it in some shape, form, or fashion. We all deploy this creative maladjustment in our lives, whether it is with our romantic partners, our boss, or our family. Over our lifetimes, we have learned to feign interest in things being "taught" to us because we either did not believe that the person teaching us could be trusted at that moment or because we were carrying so much heaviness from outside that relationship that we just could not muster the emotional bandwidth required to fully engage—or both. Or perhaps, we just literally did not care what they were talking about. Regardless, this sort of dis-associative behavior can go on for months and years at a time for even the most healthy, connected, resourced, and supported among us.

Kohl's work gets us proximate to this behavior among children in school. He is drawn to this behavioral phenomenon in particular because of the cost to the child. His work disabuses us of popular ideas that dismiss this as adolescent angst or ignorance about the long-term consequences of choosing to reject school. Instead, Kohl's discussion of willed not-learners reveals young people who are well aware that school is positioned as their best shot for access to main-stream, dominant pathways of success. Yet they still self-sabotage via an "active, often ingenious, willful rejection of even the most compassionate and well-designed teaching."[5]

Far too many children, particularly children of color and children growing up in poverty, feel the need to engage in willed not-learning in school as a mechanism of self-preservation. Kohl's final analysis of our persistent institutional failure to acknowledge, understand, and respond with care to this phenomenon is worth quoting at length:

Until we learn to distinguish not-learning from failure and to respect the truth behind this massive rejection of schooling by students from poor and oppressed communities, we will not be able to solve the major problems of education in the United States today. Risk-taking is at the heart of teaching well. That means that teachers will have to not-learn the ways of loyalty to the system and to speak out . . . We must give up looking at resistant students as failures and instead turn a critical eye toward this wealthy society and the schools that it supports.

No amount of educational research, no development of techniques or materials, no special programs or compensatory services, no restructuring or retraining of teachers will make any fundamental difference until we concede that for many students the only sane alternative to not-learning is the acknowledgment and direct confrontation of oppression—social, sexual, and economic—both in school and in society. Education built on accepting that hard truth about our society can break through not-learning and can lead students and teachers together, not to the solution of problems but to direct intelligent engagement in the struggles that might lead to solutions.[6]

The shift that Kohl insists on here demands that the top priority of schools become student well-being, particularly as it relates to the layered forms of oppression brought about by institutional and societal inequalities—awareness that any child facing daily (some even hourly) oppression from forces outside their control must have a classroom and school environment that both acknowledges and responds to that reality. This kind of responsiveness is a precondition for effective teaching with our most vulnerable children. Kohl's work reminds us that we ignore these realities of children at our own peril. We should not be shocked, stunned, or amazed when children outright reject any model of schooling that demands that they put these debilitating and, often, life-threatening realities to the side so that the business of school as we know it might continue unabated.[7]

In the absence of a "legitimate way to criticize the schooling they are subjected to or the people they are required to learn from, resistance and rebellion is stigmatized. The system's problem becomes the victim's problem," and willed not-learning becomes the primary mode of engagement for youth who are simply asking us to care more about their well-being than their test scores.[8]

CARING ABOUT, CARING FOR, AND CARING AUTHENTICALLY

Nel Noddings wrote extensively about caring, with great influence on the field of education. She presented a philosophy such that care in education became an ethical issue for her. Over the better part of thirty years, beginning with her book *Caring: A Feminine Approach to Ethics and Moral Education*, Noddings complicates simplistic and fixed notions of care (you care or you don't care) to illuminate a theory of care that honors the complexity of the classroom.[9]

Noddings's work helped us understand that the work of developing caring relationships with children is an interplay between caring *about* and caring *for*. While most of the emphasis about caring relationships is focused on caring for— that is, the direct act of caring for another person—Noddings comes to believe that caring about "must be seen as instrumental in establishing the conditions under which caring-for can flourish. Although the preferred form of caring is cared-for, caring-about can help in establishing, maintaining, and enhancing it. Those who care about others in the justice sense must keep in mind that the objective is to ensure that caring actually occurs. Caring-about is empty if it does not culminate in caring relations.[10]

Noddings notes that "caring *about*" is essential in order for widespread "caring *for*" to flourish in a classroom. This act of caring *for* rests in the concrete act of providing care for another person. But Noddings points out that this act of care must actually be understood as such by the recipient in order for it be considered caring for that person. On its face, this is such an obvious point to make, but Noddings's nuanced discussion of this distinction is essential to understanding Kohl's analysis about the conditions that drive students toward willed not-learning.[11] What Noddings points out is that simply saying that we care, or even exerting effort to show that care, does not de facto result in the recipient feeling cared for. She explains:

> Caring involves stepping out of one's own personal frame of reference into the other's. When we care, we consider the other's point of view, his objective needs, and what he expects of us. Our attention, our mental engrossment is on the cared-for, not on ourselves. Our reasons for acting, then, have to do both with the other's wants and desire and with the objective elements of his problematic situation . . . If our minds are on ourselves, however—if we have never really left our own *a priori* frame of reference—our reasons for acting point back at us and not outward to the cared-for. When we want to be thought of as caring, we often act routinely in a way that may easily secure that credit for us . . .
>
> To care is to act not by fixed rule but by affection and regard. It seems likely, then, that the actions of one-caring will be varied rather than rule-bound; that is, her actions, while predictable in a global sense, will be unpredictable in detail. Variation is to be expected if the one claiming to care really cares, for her engrossment is in the variable and never fully understood other, in the particular other, in a particular set of circumstances. Rule-bound responses in the name of caring lead us to suspect that the claimant wants most to be credited with caring.
>
> To act as one-caring, then, is to act with special regard for the particular person in a concrete situation. We act not to achieve for ourselves a commendation but to protect or enhance the welfare of the cared-for.[12]

Perhaps no research has made more important contributions to our understanding about the application of Noddings's philosophy than Angela Valenzuela's 1999 book *Subtractive Schooling*. While Noddings remains mostly silent on the role of race and culture in the ways that care is shown and received in schools, Valenzuela does not. Valenzuela looks concretely at how race and racism powerfully influence caring in schools, uncovering in practice the precise forms of "aesthetic care" that Noddings theorizes about in her work:

> [S]chools are structured around an *aesthetic* caring whose essence lies in an attention to things and ideas. Rather than centering students' learning around a moral ethic of caring that nurtures and values relationships, schools pursue a narrow, instrumentalist logic . . . the privileging of the *technical* over the *expressive* . . . Technical discourse refers to impersonal and objective language, including such terms as goals, strategies and standardized curricula, that is used in decisions made by one group for another. Expressive discourse entails "a broad and loosely defined ethic [of caring] that molds itself in situations and has proper regard for human affections, weaknesses, and anxieties."[13]

Valenzuela unmasks the schooling-education binary, which reveals itself to be highly deterministic of the qualities of teacher-student relationships inside the classroom and the institution itself. *Schooling* is the process by which students are institutionalized to accept their position in life. It emphasizes an aesthetic of care for the child and insists that the child reveal their care for school in order to receive care back from the teacher. *Education*, on the other hand, is the process by which students are given access to the tools and opportunities to transform their lives and communities. It is what Freire refers to as a problem-posing education, where the purpose of study is social justice through the development of personal agency that contributes to community actualization and cultural perpetuity.[14]

Valenzuela's research is particularly important because of the ways in which she explores how the schooling-education binary is culturally mediated. She argues that authentic care for youth of Mexican descent is an essential ingredient for disrupting patterns of Kohl's willed not-learning because it interrupts the group's experience with US schools that confirms for them that "schooling is impersonal, irrelevant, and lifeless."[15] For the youth in her study, caring is embodied in the Mexican cultural concept of *educación*, which Valenzuela describes as a "conceptually broader term than its English language cognate. It refers to the family's role of inculcating in children a sense of moral, social, and personal responsibility and serves as the foundation for all other learning. Though inclusive of formal academic training, *educación* additionally refers to competence in the social world, wherein one respects the dignity and individuality of others."[16] And so Valenzuela's work bridges Kohl's work of listening to and lifting up the voices of children who feel locked out of meaningful engagement in school, and Noddings's work on caring relationships, to offer the field the concept of "authentic care." In authentically caring relationships, caring theory is advanced to include a "pedagogical pre-occupation with questions of otherness, difference, and power" that directly confronts school processes, norms, assessments, and curriculum that remain a "sacred cow, powerful and unassessed."[17]

WHY CARING RELATIONSHIPS MATTER, AND WHAT WE SHOULD DO ABOUT IT

It would seem obvious that caring relationships matter, particularly in the classroom and most particularly with children who regularly experience the impact of radicalized inequality in our society. The previous sections of this chapter suggest that it is not as obvious as we might hope for some segments of the adult population who are in youth-serving careers. For those members of my chosen calling—those who do not care *about* or *for* the children of our communities—there is probably nothing that I can write or say that will alter their impact on our children. Simply put, if a teacher's goals do not include building deep, meaningful, and authentically caring relationships with the children they serve, then they should never be allowed to serve in vulnerable communities where the impact of uncaring adult educators is life-threatening to children. Ideally, they would be counseled out of the profession altogether.

Fortunately, over the last thirty years it has been my experience that these teachers are few and far between. The overwhelming majority of educators I encounter are working tirelessly to try to figure out how to build stronger relationships with their students because they understand intuitively that those relationships are the bedrock of success for all the other things they want to build with children. When the will is there but the results are not, the gap to be closed is the skill gap.

There are two central components to closing the skill gap as it pertains to relationships. One is understanding why relationships matter so much. While the answer here might be commonsensical, there is a growing body of research that affirms the common sense handed down to us by our elders and ancestors. This research, like those teachings, can help us develop a more nuanced and dynamic understanding of the significance of relationships. Inside the fluid subtleties of a classroom where students present a myriad of needs that are both developmental and driven by circumstance, deeper understanding means a fuller toolbox to read and react appropriately at key moments. This informed skill set is particularly important in the service of relationships with wounded youth who often do not have the time or emotional reserve to wait for moments of our convenience or the accuracy of our assessments of their needs. The more we know about relationships, the building blocks that establish and sustain them, the threats that destabilize them, and the signs of distress, the more likely we read and react appropriately with the students who need us the most.

RELATIONSHIPS, TOXIC STRESS, AND WHY ZEBRAS DON'T GET ULCERS

In 1994, Robert Sapolsky released his groundbreaking book *Why Zebras Don't Get Ulcers*.[18] Sapolsky is trained as a neuroendocrinologist and runs a neurobiology lab at Stanford University, where his research has revolutionized our scientific understanding about psychological stress, how it impacts our bodies, and how the ways we construct our lives and relationships is highly deterministic of our stress levels and the overall quality of our lives. Sapolsky is one of a host of healers, researchers, and scholars, who have been arguing that toxic stress is perhaps the most significant threat to well-being in our society.[19] Their work is elevating a critically important distinction in our understandings about stress in that they are helping us understand the difference between stress and toxic stress. This is to say that stress is a normal part of the human condition and, frankly, it is unavoidable. So, these researchers are not advocating the pursuit of a stress-free life. In fact, as David Williams at Harvard's School of Public Health puts it, there is only one group of people who live a stress-free life—dead people.[20] So, we need not rush it. Our stress-free life is coming.

I am not talking about the normal presence of stress in the lives of young people here. I am talking about the presence of chronic stress and the importance of our ability to develop and sustain meaningful relationships with young people who are immersed in that toxicity. What Sapolsky's work reveals for us is that "zebras do not get ulcers" because they do not have toxic stress in their lives. Their stress events are not chronic. A lion appears, and zebras are stressed. The zebra runs. The lion gives chase. This is a highly stressful event. Typically, the event ends fairly quickly with the zebra either avoiding or being killed by the lion. In the case of the latter outcome, the zebra is dead. No more stress. In the former outcome, where the zebra escapes the lion, the stress-induced moment is over and the zebra's bioregulatory and neurological functioning returns to normal levels. In either case, when it's over, the zebra returns to a relatively stress-free existence.

As chapter 2 discussed in some detail, the radicalized inequity that permeates our society leaves large numbers of young people running from lions most of the day and almost every day. According to Dr. Nadine Burke Harris, currently the surgeon general of California, approximately 67 percent of the US population has experienced ACEs (adverse childhood experiences).[21] The medical community now widely accepts that ACEs are one of the most significant predictors of health throughout our lives and that they deserve significantly greater and earlier attention in the lives of children because early detection and intervention are essential for a child's well-being.[22] Research into toxic stress also clearly indicates that young people of color and young people growing up in poverty are prone to higher ACE scores because of the social toxicity layered onto their childhoods by racial and economic inequality in our society.[23]

Numerous researchers have argued that one of the most important protective factors against the negative impacts of toxic stress on young people is hope, and that the most significant contributing factor in a young person's hope level is the number of caring adult relationships they have in their life.[24] S. Leonard Syme, a social epidemiologist and professor emeritus at UC Berkeley's School of Public Health, writes that we should think of hope as young people having "a sense of control of destiny."[25] Caring adult relationships, then, develop young people with an active sense of agency so that they can manage the immediate stressors in their daily life. Syme argues that recent research into the importance of hope for life outcomes is a "major breakthrough in thinking" for scholars in public health and epidemiology.[26] He attributes the genesis of this breakthrough to the groundbreaking Whitehall studies, which led to revelations that the distribution of "virtually every disease in every industrialized country in the world" was remarkably well correlated with social class.[27] For many scholars, the most likely explanation for the unequal distribution of health is the unequal distribution of hope along the social gradient. The big reveal here is that many of the health problems plaguing communities of color and communities in poverty have "unnatural causes" that are the direct result of structural inequalities in our society.[28] Thus, confirming what we have known intuitively for years; inequality is making us sick.

This is why caring relationships matter so much for youth. They quite literally play two complementary roles in the lives of children. They are medicine *and* armor. The medicine of a caring adult relationship helps children de-escalate and heal their woundedness.[29] The protective nature of caring adult relationships acts as armor against future threats to a child's wellness, which is particularly important for youth living in the chronically stressful environments created by structural inequalities.[30]

SYMPATHY VERSUS EMPATHY

Valenzuela's research on the distinction between authentically and aesthetically caring relationships is particularly important here if we are to understand how to provide youth with this medicine and armor that they need to make the leap from coping (surviving) to hoping (thriving).[31] The educational research on the significance of caring adult relationships for youth wellness is exploding, in no small part due to major upticks in attention to threats to the well-being of children.[32]

The persistent conclusion of this plethora of research into the importance of caring adult relationships for young people is that the line to be crossed for adults is the line between sympathy and empathy. Most educators are sympathetic to the woundedness of youth. They have chosen a youth-focused profession for a reason (although one sometimes wonders). So, when young people show up hurting, it is natural for educators to want to understand that suffering. But therein lies the problem. Sympathy, the search for understanding someone else's suffering, actually "drives disconnection" because, as it is cognitive in nature, it normalizes analytical distance. Sympathy is not in itself bad. But in the practice of teachers who are conditioned to have answers for their students, it lends itself to talking, fixing, and solving instead of listening, connecting, and understanding.[33]

Brené Brown's research on vulnerability has profoundly impacted discussions across fields about the distinction between sympathy and empathy.[34] In her now-famous TED Talk, one of five most viewed talks of all time (with over 45 million views), she references the work of Theresa Wiseman to define empathy.[35] Wiseman, a nurse practitioner and trainer, completed a concept analysis of empathy that heavily influenced Brown's understanding of empathy and its distinctiveness from sympathy. In her article, Wiseman traces the emergence of the concept of empathy in the English language back to psychology in the early 1900s. She links the concept to the German *Einfühlung* ("feeling into").[36] Wiseman concludes that there are four defining attributes of empathy: (1) seeing the world as others see it; (2) non-judgment; (3) understanding another's feelings; and (4) communicating the understanding of that person's feelings.[37]

Jason Thompson, a clinical psychologist who works directly with youth impacted by trauma, says that educators cannot possibly have answers for all the wounds that children are experiencing and that sometimes what a child needs is for you to become an "empathic witness in hell."[38] Brown concurs. Her research helps us understand why empathy, and not sympathy, is the bedrock of attached and caring relationships, while her TED Talk delivers an incredibly accessible description of the differences between the two:

> Empathy fuels connection. Sympathy drives disconnection . . . empathy is feeling *with* people. I always think of empathy as this sacred space, where someone's in a deep hole and they shout out from the bottom and they say, "I'm stuck. It's dark. I'm overwhelmed."
>
> And then we say "Hey!" We look and we climb down. "I know what it's like down here and you're not alone."
>
> Sympathy is [looking and shouting down the hole] "Ooh! It's bad, huh? Uh . . . no. You want a sandwich?"
>
> Empathy is a choice, and it's a vulnerable choice because in order to connect with you, I have to connect with something in myself that knows that feeling. Rarely, if ever, does an empathic response begin with "at least." And we do it all the time because someone just shared something with us that's incredibly painful and we are trying to put the silver lining around it . . . One of the things we do sometimes in the face of very difficult conversations is we try to make things better. If I share something with you that's very difficult, I'd rather you say, "I don't even know what to say right now. I'm just so glad you told me."
>
> The truth is, rarely can a response make something better. What makes something better is connection.[39]

Sympathy tracks us toward benevolence and pity because it does not lead to shared perspective or emotions. But empathy demands connection and compassion—your pain is my pain. Empathy is born out of solidarity and shared vulnerability, both of which support deeply caring and connected relationships that are critically important to the well-being of youth.[40]

Across fields, the evidence abounds for the import of educators shifting our relationships toward empathy with young people. This evidence is strongest and most profound when it comes to supporting and responding to the needs of our most wounded children. Research in psychology, neuroscience, and medicine has revealed time and time again that youth in trauma need empathic relationships.[41] Educational researchers, particularly scholars of color, have been calling for this for decades. At worst, schools and teacher training programs have roundly ignored this scholarship. At best, they have paid lip service to it while attempting to maintain a morally bankrupt system whose values and standards privilege what Manakem has called "white body supremacy" and DiAngelo has called "white fragility";[42] that is, an "all-encompassing centrality and assumed superiority of people defined and perceived as white, and the practices based on this assumption. . . . This system is based on historical and current accumulation of structural power that privileges, centralizes, and elevates white people as a group."[43] I have encountered no more than a handful of schools that seriously examine the fact that our assumptions, priorities, and practices in schools are designed to maintain and normalize this system of white supremacy.[44]

Nowhere are a teacher's and school's priorities more on display than when they are forced to respond to a young person's trauma. While I remain deeply disturbed by the persistent resistance of schools to seriously reconsider their purpose in our communities, it is refreshing that a number of schools I encounter are increasingly aware that youth trauma is pervasive and that they need to develop systems to be more responsive to it. Sadly, the overwhelming majority of these responses end up simply laying programming on top of the existing foundational priorities and practices of the school, in large part because the school does not do any purpose-driven redesign to support the implementation of these new programs. That is to say, the response presumes that the way we have set up schools is correct and that there are just a handful of young people who need "special" programming to meet their needs. Inevitably, this fails all the children in the school, most vividly those youth whom those response systems were designed to support. Schools use catchy names like RTI (response to intervention), RJ (restorative justice), and SEL (social-emotional learning) to make investments that insure nothing fundamental actually changes about the school's purpose and design. It becomes what Simmons calls "white supremacy with a hug."[45] It is a "tinkering toward utopia" that all but guarantees the same outcomes, while attending to alleviating the "white fragility" in schools that makes us feel guilty when we fail children of color.[46]

SCHOOLS (*NOT* CHILDREN) MUST CHANGE

Bruce Perry, senior fellow at the Child Trauma Academy in Houston, argues that schools need to change and that training and supporting school staff to cultivate empathic relationships is the starting point for shifting what is happening for vulnerable youth in schools. In his first book, *The Boy Who Was Raised as a Dog*, he writes: "Our educational system has focused nearly obsessively on cognitive development and almost completely ignored children's emotional and physical needs . . . our educational system and our society's general disrespect for the importance of relationships is undermining the development of empathy."[47] He goes on at length, stressing the importance of a purposeful reorganization of schools to place much greater emphasis on the development of healthy relationships. He compares the need for empathy and the development of empathy to language because, like language, empathy is a fundamental element of human well-being and it must be learned.[48]

Sadly, the group of young people most in need of this cultural shift in schools are also the ones who are least likely to experience it. The young people who come to school the most wounded and

the most traumatized are often also the ones who are the most entrenched in our nation's systemic inequity, and therefore they are
also the most likely to be re-exposed to trauma. They *need* schools
to be better. They need schools to be a place where their relationships with adults give them the medicine of love, time, and patience.
They need schools to be a place where they can recharge their armor
and feel better protected from a society that has devalued them and
taught them that they are undeserving. Perry, like Maestro Jerry
Tello, a founder of the National Compadres Network, has spent the
better part of his adult life healing wounded children.[49] Perry's and
Tello's books should be mandatory reading for anyone working in
schools because, as Perry and Szalavitz point out:

> Traumatized children tend to have overreactive stress responses
> and . . . these can make them aggressive, impulsive and needy . . .
> Before they can make any kind of lasting change at all in their be-
> havior, they need to feel safe and loved. Unfortunately, however,
> many of the treatment programs and other interventions aimed
> at them get it backwards: they take a punitive approach and hope
> to lure children into good behavior by restoring love and safety
> only if the children start acting "better." While such approaches
> may temporarily threaten children into doing what adults want,
> they can't provide the long-term internal motivation that will ul-
> timately help them control themselves better and become more
> loving toward others.
>
> Troubled children are in some kind of pain—and pain makes
> people irritable, anxious and aggressive. Only patient, loving,
> consistent care works; there are no short-term miracle cures. This
> is as true for a child of three or four as it is for a teenager.[50]

Tello describes this pain given to children as an attack on their
sacredness:

We see manifestations of this when someone is treated in a negative way, and then processes this as feeling unwanted, or perceives that [they do] not meet the expectations of family, community, or society. The experience can definitely impact a child, or adult in a painful way throughout life . . . The feeling early on of being unworthy, unloved, or not meeting the expectations among basic circles of relations, can affect a person's self-worth, self-esteem, and long-term sense of sacredness and sacred purpose.

 . . . [G]etting a formal education is very important. However, formal education as presently structured does not provide a path to overall human development which will enable a person to deal with challenges posed by a modern society. In fact, today's dominant culture and societal norms reinforce patterns and habits that often pull people away from their relationships and sacred purpose. These norms often encourage habits and practices that are more materialistic and less focused on true happiness and harmony in life.[51]

As troubling as it can be to think about where we are as a society and where we are in schools, I remain eminently hopeful because I am around children and community-responsive educators every day. When you spend time around children, especially in communities like mine where there is so much unearned suffering, and you watch their unrequited joy and hopefulness, you cannot help but be a believer that we can do better. And when you see how hard educators are working to try to get it right and when you see all the systemic obstacles to them delivering on the promise that our youth deserve, you cannot help but be legitimately angry and passionately driven to bang on the system to change.

What follows is a set of concrete examples of the practice of people and places that are actually delivering on the promise of relationships, the first of the three domains (relationships, relevance, and responsibility) of community-responsive pedagogy.[52] The intention of providing these examples is threefold. First, seeing is believing. I believe in the importance and impact of community responsiveness because I have seen it in my own practice and countless times in my research. Second, I want everyone who reads this book to know that this is not pie-in-the-sky theory that falls flat when we move it from the whiteboard to the classroom. This is what works. We know it works, and we have concrete examples of how and why it works. Thirdly, the examples are meant to be beacons of light when the darkness comes. This work is so, so hard. For those who have never taught, I cannot possibly explain the complexity of the classroom. For those who have never led a school, I cannot possibly explain the enormity of that challenge. The existence of exemplars provides an important touch point for practitioners because it reminds us of what is possible, while also reminding us that that possibility is achieved not when everything is as we drew it up, but when we are able to find meaning in the mess.

CLOSING THE KNOWING DOING GAP: WHAT DO RELATIONSHIPS LOOK LIKE IN PRACTICE?

Mr. Kanamori's "Children Full of Life"

The documentary film *Children Full of Life* follows the fourth-grade class of Toshiro Kanamori over the course of a year.[53] The class goal for the year is to learn how to live a happy life and how to care for other people. The film documents Kanamori's pedagogy with his students as they pursue this goal and it is split up into five sections to explore their journey (Feelings, Bullying, Challenging the Teacher, Death and Uncertainty, and The Letter—An Act of Compassion).

Each day in Kanamori's class, three students read aloud letters they have written in their notebooks. These "notebook letters" are written to the other students in the class and are true reflections of the emotions and feelings that they are experiencing that day. As the teacher, Kanamori is reading all of them, which gives him tremendous insight into his students' lives, but it is in the students' sharing with their peers that the class goal becomes more attainable. The film is an incredible exploration of the complexity of the class-room and the swings that happen in the social dynamics between students and between students and the teacher. As a teacher, I appreciate much about the film, but what is particularly important to me is that the film reveals that even the most accomplished teachers struggle. This is important insight for educators who believe that ef-fective teachers have some pixie dust that we sprinkle on youth that magically generates docility and compliance, allowing us to skate through the day unscathed and with flawless delivery of our lessons. It is my experience, buoyed by what I saw in Kanamori's class, that all teachers have similar conflicts with students—what differentiates teachers is their humility and empathy in their response to those challenges.

The road to these responses is paved daily by our pedagogy. The more that empathy sits at the core of our daily lessons, the more likely it is that our students model this behavior back to us and the more likely it is that they will be receptive to it in times of conflict and distress. This is modeled beautifully in the first segment of the film, when a student named Ren returns to class after missing four days because his grandmother died. The narrator explains that "in his notebook, Ren writes about the death, the funeral, his loss" and Kanamori has him share his letter with the class. The students in the class did not know why Ren was away, and as the camera pans the room, it is visibly apparent that his peers are moved by his words and connecting with his loss. He ends with "Grandma was gone. I was sad." Children who share a connection with Ren's letter are asked to raise their hand, stand up as a collective, and if they are so moved, they can share their stories. What happens next is the shared vulnerability that psychologists and neurologists talk about when true empathy occurs.

One young girl shares that on the night before her birthday, her grandfather died in his sleep. She laments not being able to say goodbye to him and in the middle of her next sentence she breaks down, puts her face into her hands, and begins weeping in front of her peers. Silence ensues as other students get choked up. Then Mifuyu, another girl in the class, speaks up. The whole time she is wiping tears from her eyes and battling through her own sobbing:

MIFUYU: When I was four years old, my father died. I wanted to write about it in class, but I couldn't. Even though I was only four when my father died, I already knew that people died.

NARRATOR: She'd been afraid to talk about her father. She didn't want to seem different. She paid a price.

MIFUYU: But I couldn't stop crying. I couldn't speak on the phone. And when I heard that story, I felt so sad.

NARRATOR: Now, at last, she feels safe enough to talk about her missing parent.

What happens next is pure pedagogical genius on the part of Kanamori. Kanamori has known Mifuyu's history. He has watched her childhood trauma stifle her engagement and performance as a student and he has been hoping the space would open up for her to share and begin healing with the class. That moment has arrived, and as she is speaking, Kanamori repositions himself behind Mifuyu in a show of solidarity and support for her sharing. He kneels down so that he is at her level and he places his hand on her shoulder as she buries her face in her hands and sobs. He says, "Today, Mifuyu told us her story. It's hard keeping it locked away, isn't it? That's why I hoped she'd talk about her father. I knew she'd feel better once she came out with it. And it was Ren's letter that gave her the courage."

The camera pans to Ren, and you can see in his expression a satisfaction that his writing and his courage to share his writing about his loss has created a healing space for Mifuyu and his peers. Kanamori gives the class time to process all that they are feeling, and the visuals of that are stunning and moving. The children begin healing each other. They slide up next to their peers who are hurting and they comfort them, providing proximity and reassuring rubs on the back.

One child, Yoenomoto, is so impacted by the emotion in the room that he leaves and goes to the bathroom to cry. Another student follows him and then comes back to tell Kanamori, which leads to the following exchange between Yoenomoto and Kanamori in the bathroom:

NARRATOR: Yoenomoto is the class spark plug. High-energy. Charming. Now he's remembering the death of his grandmother.

KANAMORI [*his hand gently patting the child's cheek to dry his tears*]: It brought it all back did it?

[*Child, sobbing, nods his head*].

KANAMORI [*his arm around the student, gently hugging him as he starts to sob*]: That's good. That's excellent. But now, let's go eat.

Kanamori is interviewed following this incredible series of moments with his students (best experienced by watching the film).[54] He reflects: "Empathy is the greatest thing. There's an expression I love: 'Let people live in your heart.' There's no limit on numbers. They tell the stories, and everyone shares their feelings. When people really listen, they live in your heart forever. That's the great significance of these notebook letters."

Following Kanamori's interview, Mifuyu shows back up to class with a framed picture of a model her father designed for a parade before he died. She hangs the picture in the front of the class and presents her father, and her new self, to the class. Her healing with her community has begun in earnest.

The story of Kanamori and his fourth-grade class is compelling on many levels, but it is still the story of the exceptional individual teacher. His pedagogy, while highly effective for his classroom, does not necessarily (or easily) transfer to schoolwide practices. All over the country, there are examples of incredible educators and school spaces that are truly transformative. It is important that we keep saying that and that we make a greater investment in supporting and studying those spaces because those are the "hope dealers" for our youth and for our field.[55] Every day, these hope dealers are battling the dope dealers competing for the hearts and minds of our children. And when I say "dope dealers," I am not talking about our cousins standing on the street corners pushing nickel and dime bags. I am talking about textbook companies, testing paradigms, toxic school climates and cultures, and media messages that teach our children to hate themselves for the color of their skin, the texture of their hair, the language they speak, the lands of their origin, the neighborhoods they come from, the families that raise them, and the ancestors that dreamed of them. Those are the dope dealers that hope dealers must battle every day, because if you pump that self-hate into the veins and brains of young people long enough, that is when they end up on the trigger of a gun or in the suck of the streets trying to make dollars out of nickels and dimes. There is no way you pick up a gun and point it at someone who looks just like you and let the hammer fly unless you hate what you see when you look in the mirror. Hope dealers save lives, and we need to understand their work with much greater urgency so that we stop losing our children. Part of this process of understanding demands that we also sort out how to turn those spaces into places. That is, how do we make the experience that Kanamori delivers to his students an institutional practice? In my experience, finding examples at the institutional level are incredibly rare. I have read about a few. I have seen even fewer.

What follows is the story of Lincoln High School. The work that they took on is an important lesson for us as we consider how to expand the hope dealing that our youth experience from the classroom to the entire school.

The Case of Lincoln High School

In 2010, three years into his principalship at Lincoln High School, in Walla Walla, Washington, Jim Sporleder chose to change.[56] Sporleder, a veteran school administrator with twenty-five years of experience under his belt, was known for his strong rapport with students. He doled out "discipline with dignity."[57] He took the job at Lincoln late in his career after reading a report about the school that dubbed it a dumping ground for the most challenging students in the area. Lincoln High was widely considered the last stop for youth on their way to dropping out, prison, or premature death.

Sporleder was struggling and found himself suspending and expelling students right and left in reaction to over six hundred disciplinary referrals from teachers in a school of only fifty students. Prompted by a colleague from the Children's Resilience Initiative (CRI), Sporleder attended a training led by John Medina, a developmental molecular biologist and author of *Brain Rules*.[58] Stevens explains that Medina "drilled a hole in Sporleder's brain and dropped this in: Severe and chronic trauma (such as living with an alcoholic parent, or watching in terror as your mom gets beat up) causes toxic stress in kids. Toxic stress damages kids' brains. When trauma launches kids into flight, fight, or fright mode, they cannot learn. It is physiologically impossible."[59]

Sporleder says that Medina explained the science of trauma in way that made it accessible to him as an educator and school administrator. Stevens's article about the transformation at Lincoln High School highlights what she calls the "dark underbelly of school discipline," explaining that there simply is no research to suggest that suspensions work for schools. School discipline data shows that suspensions fail both the school and the child being suspended. A 2011 National Education Policy Center (NEPC) report revealed how suspensions have skyrocketed, particularly for youth of color, since the 1970s. According to the report, even when controlling for race and poverty, out-of-school suspensions correlate with lower achievement for the school as a whole. For the individual child being suspended, the results are tragic. California Chief Justice Tani Cantil-Sakauye reported that "one suspension triples the likelihood of a juvenile justice contact within that year and one suspension doubles the likelihood of repeating the grade."[60]

Sporleder, with the support of Teri Barila from CRI, brought Natalie Turner from Washington State University's Area Health Education Center to work with the staff to develop Lincoln High School into a trauma-free school. Turner's two rules for working with wounded youth are:

1. Take nothing a raging kid says personally. Really. Act like a duck: let the words roll off your back like drops of water.
2. Don't mirror the kid's behavior. Take a deep breath. Wait for the storm to pass, and then ask something along the lines of: "Are you okay? Did something happen to you that's bothering you? Do you want to talk about it?"[61]

Turner brought a whole host of resources to Lincoln that allowed them to completely change their school discipline system from a system of punishment to a system of care. [62] This does not mean that there are not consequences for negative or dangerous student behavior, but that is not the starting point of response to their youth when they are in crisis. The starting point is making sure that that child knows that the adults in the school genuinely care about their well-being *first*.

Turner's model focused on three units of change for Lincoln: the classroom, the principal, and staff meetings. In the classroom, teachers become "detectives" whose focus is on sleuthing out what is going in students' lives that might be causing negative behaviors, instead of calculating "what type of punishment to mete out."[63] If an issue is escalated to the principal and students show up in Sporleder's office in what he calls the "red zone," the impact of his response is as much about what he does *not* do as it is about what he *does* do:

> He does not yell. He doesn't roll his eyes. There's no body language that says "I can't stand you kids," because he actually thinks the world of them.
> "Let's meet tomorrow. You're going to take the rest of the day and night to process this."
> Sometimes Sporleder has found himself in the red zone, and tells the kids, "I'm in the red. I don't want to make any decisions that could come from my own anger or stress. Let's take a break and meet later."[64]

This approach is nearly perfectly aligned with the recommendations coming from some of the nation's leading experts on responding to youth trauma.[65] According to Perry and Szalavitz:

> One of the greatest lessons I've learned in my work is the importance of simply taking the time, before doing anything else, to

pay attention and listen. Because of the mirroring neurobiology of our brains, one of the best ways to help someone else be calm and centered is to calm and center ourselves first—and then just pay attention.

. . . [T]he more you try to see the world from the child's point of view and the safer you make [them] feel, the better [their] behavior is likely to be and the more likely you are to find ways of further improving it.[66]

The science used to justify Perry's approach is not new to communities of color. Our elders and ancestors have been calling for more culturally responsive, kinder, and more caring adult behaviors since policy mandated our children attend public schools. The results at Lincoln as a result of these change in approach have been shockingly good, but they should not be shocking to us at all. It is simply another validation of the wisdom of our grandmothers, now backed by the institutional support of research in medicine, psychology and neuroscience.[67]

And so Sporleder reports that more often than not, the students circle back to him the next day and tell him they have apologized and worked out a solution with the teacher with whom they had the conflict. In the rare cases where the students and teachers are not able to sort it out themselves, then Sporleder might refer students to a space where they can get additional emotional support, counseling, and support with their coursework so that they do not fall behind. According to Sporleder, he doesn't "have kids arguing about the consequences anymore."

Staff meetings at Lincoln have also changed. Rather than staff dialogue focusing on the problems that students are causing at the school, the conversations focus on what is happening with students who are struggling, and plans are developed to better support those students. According to teachers, self-regulation among students has dramatically improved, major emotional outbursts have decreased, and the way students interact with one another has qualitatively improved.

This is no panacea. Lincoln still has its challenges. But its work is being lifted up here because it is an example of what is possible when a school dramatically changes its purpose. Lincoln's educators did not add on a new program for "at-risk," "troubled," "at-promise," "high needs" students. They did not create an equity office. They did not hire an equity officer. They did not try to figure out how to fix the "broken" children. They finally stopped locating the problem in the children and their families to realize that the real problem lay in the way the institution treated and responded to the children. No program was going to transform Lincoln, only people could do that and the only possibility for that was the repurposing of the entire project from the foundation on up. Lincoln repurposed itself. The grownups chose to be grownups, heeding James Baldwin's challenge quoted earlier in this chapter and taking a hard look at themselves. They began to see the wisdom of one of my Maestros, Jerry Tello, who taught me that "wounded children speak the most truth, and we resent them for it." Educators at Lincoln replaced correction with curiosity, seeking first to understand the truth telling that the children were doing when they disconnected and disrupted the flow of an institution that claimed to care about them but seemed hell-bent on breaking them.

The educators at Lincoln heeded the wisdom of my mother, whose favorite *dicho* for me as a child was, "Boy, if it ain't broke, don't fix it." The children of Lincoln were not broken. None of our children are broken. The society that we have built for them, and the institutions that uphold it, are what are in need of fixing. The lesson of Lincoln is that transformation is possible when, and only when, we are willing to repurpose schools. Lincoln made community-responsive relationships the core of everything that they do. The results are undeniable and everyone (teachers, students, families, and the community) are the beneficiaries.

RELATIONSHIPS PAVE THE WAY TO EQUITY

Whether it is the efforts of an exceptional teacher or the collective commitment of an entire institution, both of these examples are evidence of the power of relationships to transform the lives of wounded children. As Perry and Szalavitz put it:

> What maltreated and traumatized children most need is a healthy community to buffer the pain, distress and loss caused by their earlier trauma. What works to heal them is anything that increases the number and quality of a child's relationships. What helps is consistent, patient, repetitive loving care. And I should add, what doesn't work is well-intended poorly trained . . . "professionals" rushing in after a traumatic event, or coercing children to "open up" or "get out their anger."[68]

Every year, educators are bombarded with the latest and greatest programmatic and curricular fixes for all things that ail classrooms and schools. The success of these fixes often rises and falls along the barometer of relationships between child and educator. Countless studies of effective educators and schools highlight the strength of relationships between adults and children as the secret sauce in successful teaching and learning environments. Outside of educational research, there is widespread cross-disciplinary research (neuroscience, social epidemiology, psychology, public health, medicine) supporting the central importance of attached, caring, and meaningful adult-child relationships as the foundation of a healthy learning environment for children. This fact is likely unsurprising to laypeople, and if you have taught in a classroom for a day, then you certainly know it to be true. Yet schools continue to create and replicate conditions that strain, and sometimes toxify, relationships between adults and children, between children, and between adults themselves.

Joan Cone, a longtime classroom teacher and mentor of mine, once told me that schools must be better than society if our society is ever going to improve. The truth is that schools are often social mirrors and, unless we heed Joan's advice, we stand little chance of becoming the society we aim to be. Nowhere is the gap between our rhetoric and our reality more clearly on display than in the apartheid-like data we see when we compare the school experiences and outcomes of children in poverty and children of color with those of their more affluent white counterparts. The decades-long handwringing and blatant dishonesty around the complete and abject failure of our nation's public schools to meet the needs of our most vulnerable children is shameful and a profound indictment of our national moral integrity.

Luckily for us, it does not have to be this way. In both research and practice, we have strong evidence about what it takes to build caring relationships. In the last decade, research in neuroscience, medicine, and social epidemiology has exploded as connections between inequality, toxic stress, and poor health have been clearly mapped and inextricably linked. This research has also illuminated the profoundly positive effects when children have long-term access to wellness. And it reveals the potential of schools to be a massive accelerant in the development of a generation of children who in fairly short order have the potential to bring us back from the edge of social apartheid to a place of greater wellness, democracy, and peace. At the heart of this effort will be a commitment to equitable and community-responsive relationships in schools and classrooms where children who come to school with the least will get the most; this happens by virtue of the fact that when we commit to equity, we commit to giving children *what* they need, *when* they need it.

CHAPTER 5

RELEVANCE

What Are We Teaching Our Children?

"Then said a teacher, Speak to us of Teaching. And he said: No man can reveal to you aught but that which already lies half asleep in the dawning of your knowledge. The teacher who walks in the shadow of the temple, among his followers, gives not of his wisdom but rather of his faith and his lovingness. If he is indeed wise he does not bid you enter the house of his wisdom, but rather leads you to the threshold of your own mind.

The astronomer may speak to you of his understanding of space, but he cannot give you his understanding. The musician may sing to you of the rhythm which is in all space, but he cannot give you the ear which arrests the rhythm nor the voice that echoes it. And he who is versed in the science of numbers can tell of the regions of weight and measure, but he cannot conduct you thither.

For the vision of one man lends not its wings to another man."

—Kahlil Gibran, "On Teaching"

If we get relationships right, we should also be asking ourselves: *What* we are teaching our children, *how* are we teaching it, and *why* we are teaching it? Choices about what will be taught to our children and, ergo, what will *not* be taught are value laden and politically charged. The curriculum and pedagogy we use with children has a profound influence on their thinking and the value systems they develop. These, in turn, significantly color the direction of our society. If we do not change *what* we teach, *how* we teach it, and *why* we teach it, then we cannot fairly expect outcomes to change for those children who find themselves perpetually disconnected from school.

There is a clear and measurable shift in experience, engagement, and outcomes that occurs when children find relevance in what is being taught. This chapter explores research across fields that helps us understand the reason for this shift and the clear developmental logic sequence that unfolds for children when this connection happens. Culturally and community-affirming schools and classrooms increase knowledge of self and self-esteem.[1] As Maslow and so many others have established, self-esteem is the window into self-actualization, which has long been held up as a defining characteristic of school (and life) success.[2] This affirmation for any child, but particularly for children whose social and cultural identities locate them on the margins of society, triggers what psychologists call the *Pygmalion effect,* a recurring cycle of affirming self-talk that increases self-confidence, resilience, and positive outcomes.

More recent research on children who successfully navigate toxic stress in their lives reveals a clear correlation between their self-esteem (regarded as "agency") and what social epidemiologists like Leonard Syme and psychologists like Charles Snyder are measuring as children's hope levels.[3] As cultural relevance elevates a child's hope level, research reveals that this is a powerful antidote to what psychologist Claude Steele calls "stereotype threat."[4] Steele's work serves as one of the most compelling analyses we have to explain why children of color, regardless of social class, continue to underperform in school in comparison to their white peers. Steele's work also holds great promise for helping us understand how to change that pattern. Carol Dweck has argued that the key to interrupting these long-standing patterns of unequal outcomes is the cultivation of a "growth mindset."[5]

I am regularly in school districts all over the country that lay claim to commitments of cultural relevance, cultural responsiveness, and/or cultural sustainability.[6] Each of these approaches can be thought of as steps toward being community responsive.[7] While I am not particularly fond of checklists as a way to move toward any of these approaches, I will provide one here as a starting point for a discussion on relevance in schools.

If an educational space is committed to being relevant to the youth being served there, then we should see a consistent centering of students' lives, communities, families, and ethnic, cultural, and linguistic histories in every aspect of the space, climate, culture, pedagogy and curriculum. At a very basic level of logic, this should make sense to even the most novice of educators. Yet when we visit classrooms and common spaces where there is an expressed commitment to relevance, the rhetoric and the reality are often starkly different. At best, modes of interaction, procedures, signage, institutional structures, curriculum, and assessments pay passing homage to the profound histories and cultures carried into the buildings every day by the children who attend. On average, most schools and classrooms fall back onto modes of dominant cultural reproduction, steeping their systems and practices inside the very values that all but guarantee the continued marginalization of large portions of their students and families.

The reasons behind these decisions are surely varied and complex. It is my belief that at least some of what sits underneath the incongruity of a rhetoric of cultural relevance and a reality of dominant cultural reproduction is a lack of awareness about what community responsiveness looks like, why it matters so much, and what it takes to achieve it. Research across fields shows that connection matters, and that connection happens when the things we are learning have clear and obvious relevance to our lives and our passions. The lives and passions of those who are doing the worst in schools right now have rarely mattered much to those schools. In fact, much of the design history and practices of schools serving racially and economically vulnerable youth are situated in a commitment to, at best, altering the cultural lives and passions of children and, at worst, expunging them. Both of these perspectives are driven by frameworks and sensibilities that deem the cultural histories and identities of vulnerable children as deficient and presume the dominant culture to be preferable and superior.

The origins of this investment in altering students, instead of developing them, is imbued in the history of boarding schools for Western Indigenous peoples. In the mid-late 1800s, the US government was growing increasingly concerned with their inability to bring the "wilder tribes" under its control. In the 1850 *Annual Report of the Commissioner of Indian Affairs*, then Commissioner Luke Lea wrote that certain tribes had an "insatiable passion for war" and that it was "necessary that they be placed in positions where they can be controlled."[8] Lea's predecessor, Charles E. Mix, had some thirty years earlier provided for the establishment of "manual labor schools" on reservations to minimize mixing with whites and to make sure that Indigenous children learned the civilized "habits of industry" in place of their savage culture.[9] The policies and practices born out of these sentiments gave way to congressional creation of the Indian Peace Commission in 1867 chaired by Nathaniel Taylor, who told Crow Indians that "we will send you teachers for your children."[10] The prevailing educational policies were full-blown commitments to destroying the language, values, and cultural practices of Indigenous children and replacing them with English monolingualism and white cultural practices and beliefs. Quoting the 1868

Indian Peace Commission report: "Through sameness of language is produced sameness of sentiment and thought; customs and habits are moulded [*sic*] and assimilated in the same way, and thus in the process of time the differences producing trouble would have been gradually obliterated."[11]

The pattern of public schools being used as cultural erasers is not unique to the experiences of Indigenous communities. The depth of literature naming US public schools as sites of deculturation and suffering for children of color is shockingly deep and persistent, dating back to Carter G. Woodson's *The Mis-Education of the Negro* in 1933.[12] Since then, scholars have been pointing out Black youth experiences that reflect structural designs for isolation.[13] Similar literature exists for the experiences of Latinx youth.[14]

WHY DO COMMUNITY AND CULTURAL RESPONSIVENESS MATTER?

Just as we find a river of research, deep and wide, to support the commonsensical notion that relationships matter in teaching, the literature does not disappoint as it speaks to the importance of community and cultural responsiveness. Let me start by saying that I include cultural responsiveness only because of how nescient present-day discourse is about community-responsive pedagogy. One cannot be community responsive without also being culturally responsive because to have a pedagogy that reflects the community, one would certainly consider the culture of the community in that design. Dr. Allyson Tintiangco-Cubales and myself, among others, have pushed this concept of community responsiveness because of the problematics that have developed with culturally responsive pedagogy—specifically the culture piece of it.[15] We have watched as schools across the nation, in search of shortcuts to cultural responsiveness, have essentialized culture and used it as a proxy for race. In other words, schools all over the country have sought out programs that showed promise in another community with a similar racial demographic and then attempted to copy that program over into their community because they had a similar racial demographic of students.

Of course, these efforts nearly always fail because successful efforts at cultural responsiveness are, in their essence, community responsive. That is to say, effective educators understand that their success is dependent on a commitment to reflecting the unique unfolding of the racialized culture of their students as it relates to that particular community. The lack of understanding about this fact is absolutely stunning to me. How could a predominantly Black school in Chicago think to teach about the Black Panthers in the same way as a predominantly Black school in Oakland, the birthplace of the Panthers? This does not mean that both schools should not teach about the Panthers, but the teachings would need to reflect the culture and history of the community. While community-responsive educators would surely see this difference, it has not been my experience that this seemingly obvious distinction is given proper attention in the practice of a wide swath of educators who aim to be culturally responsive.

Thus the shift to community responsiveness, which insists that educators begin with attention to the community where they are doing the work and build out curriculum and pedagogical norms from there. What follows is a breakdown of a clear logic sequence that emerges in the research about why community and cultural responsiveness matters so much, particularly for students who come from outside the dominant culture (see figure 5.1).

DEVELOPING KNOWLEDGE OF SELF

Dee and Penner, in their study of the Ethnic Studies program in San Francisco Unified Schools, found that daily access to a curriculum and pedagogy that focused on knowledge of self had a strongly

FIGURE 5.1 Community and cultural responsiveness logic sequence

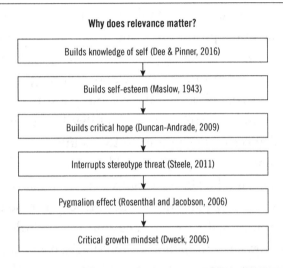

Why does relevance matter?

Builds knowledge of self (Dee & Pinner, 2016)

Builds self-esteem (Maslow, 1943)

Builds critical hope (Duncan-Andrade, 2009)

Interrupts stereotype threat (Steele, 2011)

Pygmalion effect (Rosenthal and Jacobson, 2006)

Critical growth mindset (Dweck, 2006)

Sources: Thomas Dee and Emily Penner, "The Causal Effects of Cultural Relevance: Evidence from an Ethnic Studies Curriculum" (Stanford University Center for Education Policy Analysis (CEPA) Working Paper 2016: 16–01); Abraham Maslow, "A Theory of Human Motivation," *Psychological Review* 50 (1943): 6.; Jeff Duncan-Andrade, "Note to Educators: Hope Required When Growing Roses in Concrete," *Harvard Education Review* 79, no. 2 (2009): 1–13; Claude M. Steele, *Whistling Vivaldi* (New York: W. W. Norton, 2011); Robert Rosenthal and Lenore Jacobson, *Pygmalion in the Classroom* (Carmarthen, UK: Crown House, 2003); Carol S. Dweck, *Mindset: The New Psychology of Success* (New York: Ballantine Books, 2006).

correlated, if not causal, impact on student achievement.[16] This is a profound research claim. In our field, we will always struggle to identify causal because there are so many factors outside of a teacher's control that can be additive or disruptive to student well-being. What this research does reveal is that community-responsive curriculum and pedagogy can literally change the outcome trajectory for students, particularly for those students whom public schools have been failing.

For neuroscientists and social psychologists, this revelation is totally unsurprising. There is clear evidence in those fields that connection matters. A community-responsive curriculum ensures that students see themselves in the instructional material and approach on a regular basis. This is particularly important for young people who do not receive this kind of validation about their personal value and the value of the people from whom they come in the larger society. For many of the young people who are struggling in school, the messages in the broader society are not affirming. They are bombarded with social, political, and economic constructs that demean their cultural and ancestral heritage and that lift up and affirm the cultural and ancestral practices of WASP culture.

This is not to say that white children should not be affirmed. All children should be affirmed. But when the broader society and the majority of school curriculum and instruction are so profoundly focused on affirming the dominant culture, there is little chance that our society grows into the pluralistic multiracial democracy we could become. Every decision made about curriculum is a double-edged sword. When we choose what we are including, we are also choosing what we are excluding. This is not commonly noted in discussions of curriculum, and so it becomes what Bowles and Gintis refer to as the "hidden curriculum."[17] We are responsible for acknowledging that we are teaching students based on what we *exclude*, and what we are teaching them is that those things are not as important as the things we choose to include. When the things we exclude are the very things that would otherwise be affirming of students' cultural identities, we are undermining the potential of schools to develop young people with a strong awareness and connection to a knowledge of self.

As scholars have asserted the central role that race (and racism) often plays in these decisions, research has exploded in the examinations of the role of Ethnic Studies curriculum and pedagogy to close this gap for students.[18] Dee and Penner's research on the significant role that curriculum and pedagogy play in this process is just the latest in discussions about the importance of putting the child and the community at the center of curriculum design that dates all the way back to Dewey's *The Child and the Curriculum*.[19]

GROWING SELF-ESTEEM

Students with greater knowledge of self trend toward higher self-esteem. The discussion of self-esteem has come up earlier in this book through references to Maslow's hierarchy of needs, where self-esteem is the window into self-actualization. As educators, we aspire to grow young people who self-actualize in their learning and in their broader life endeavors, yet there is virtually no attention paid to the fact that self-esteem is the precursor to self-actualization. Our public schools have made little to no investment to design curriculum, pedagogy, and assessment to centralize self-esteem (self-love) for students generally, and even less has been done to invest in building the self-esteem of children of color. For white children whose value to the larger society is already affirmed by the very design of our larger social norms and structures, the absence of this focus in the curriculum is less interruptive of their well-being. To the degree that curriculum and pedagogy do bolster self-esteem for children, it is most commonly through the lens of white, male, heterosexual, and European cultural norms, values, and histories.

There is no debate in the research community that curriculum and pedagogical choices are heavily determinant (perhaps even causal) of outcomes for students of color in schools. What we now understand at much greater depth is *why* those choices matter so much, and it is because of the chain reaction that is set off when curriculum, pedagogy, culture, and climate are affirming (or not) to children. As they are exposed to schools that both emphasize and value their cultural identities and histories, their knowledge of self is deepened and this grows their self-esteem.

BUILDING CRITICAL HOPE

As a child's self-esteem rises, so does their hope level. According to S. Leonard Syme, professor emeritus at UC Berkeley's School of Public Health, recent research into the development of hope in youth shows the most promise for creating classroom spaces where students are thriving.[20] Syme describes hope as a sense of "control of destiny"— an actively present sense of agency to manage the immediate stressors in one's daily life; and he calls the research community's growing attention to strategies for cultivating hope in youth facing intense social stressors a "major breakthrough in thinking."[21]

Renowned positive psychologist Charles Snyder's hope theory and Children's Hope Scale identified two key components to hope: (1) identifying pathways toward a desired goal, and (2) motivating oneself to begin and sustain goal-directed behavior (agency). Snyder calls this "hope theory," and numerous studies show hope to be one of the best indicators we have for predicting student resiliency, success, and well-being.[22]

One would be hard-pressed to find a successful educator who would disagree with the importance of developing hope in the lives of young people as a principal pathway to raising engagement and achievement. Despite this acknowledgment by our most accomplished teachers, it is my sense that very few teacher-development programs explicitly discuss hope as a pedagogical concept. The insistence by educational policy makers (particularly since NCLB in 2001) that educational practice by guided by "scientifically based research" presents an opportunity to change this trend if teacher education has the foresight to use recent breakthroughs in research on the social indicators of health, specifically the significance of hope among youth, in that research.[23]

In my previous work, I describe a commitment to cultivating hope as a bedrock principle for effective classroom pedagogy and school culture.[24] In that work, I examine theory and research on hope to develop an educator's framework on critical hope, making the argument that our nation expends a good deal of effort trying to avoid what Carl Jung referred to as "legitimate suffering," or the naturally occurring pain that comes along with the human experience.[25] Instead, we permit the stockpiling of resources in privileged portions of the population so that they may avoid as much suffering as possible, while simultaneously supporting political and economic policies that isolate the unnatural causes of socially toxic environments onto others.[26] This creates undeserved suffering among the nation's most vulnerable populations of children, and then we expend tremendous effort ducking, dodging, and delegitimizing it in our school system. In the face of these conditions, committing to building critical hope in our youth is a bold stance of solidarity with vulnerable communities, confronting the burden of their undeserved suffering as a primary responsibility of our teaching practice.

An educator committed to building critical hope also defies the dominant ideology of defense, entitlement, and preservation of privileged bodies at the expense of the policing, disposal, and dispossession of marginalized "others." We cannot treat our students as "other people's children"—their pain *is* our pain.[27] False hope would have us believe in individualized notions of success and suffering, but critical hope demands that we reconnect to the collective by struggling alongside of one another, sharing in the victories *and* the pain. This solidarity is the essential ingredient for "radical healing," and healing is an often overlooked factor for raising hope and achievement in schools.[28]

There is an inescapable challenge before us as educators, and it is often misunderstood. Too many of us try to create school spaces that are safe from righteous rage—or worse, we design plans to "weed out" children who display it. The question we should be grappling with is not how to manage students with these emotions, but how we will help students channel them. The inevitable moments of despair and rage that wounded youth feel are understandable and an "appropriate response to an absurd situation."[29] West argues that youth "are saying they want to see a sermon, not hear one. They want an example. They want to be able to perceive in palpable concrete form how these channels will allow them to vent their rage constructively and make sure that it will have an impact."[30]

If the accumulation of negative stressors caused by inequality is like having a boot on your neck, then coping strategies are the strengthening of one's neck to handle the pressure of the boot. This is an important strategy, one in which many of our students are well practiced. However, as suggested by the expanding research on the social indicators of health, a lifetime of coping atrophies the body and can deteriorate into hopelessness.[31] To capitalize on students' coping resiliency without trapping them under that boot means engaging the project of moving from coping to hoping. When adults in schools *show* the sermon with how we live our lives, rather than just *preaching* it as a way for our students to live their lives, students see living proof of the transition from just coping to a life of hoping.

The way I have taken on this challenge as an educator is by thinking about schools and classrooms as micro-ecosystems. Ecologists would tell us that to build a healthy micro-ecosystem, we need to understand the principle of interdependency—in short, both pain and healing are transferable from person to person inside school spaces.

I'd like to use two metaphors here to help educators understand how I think about this idea of school spaces as micro-ecosystems. The first is an allegory presented by Camara Jones to provide a commonsense analysis of the health impacts of racism. Jones describes two flower boxes that sat outside her newly purchased home. One box was empty and the other was filled with soil. Jones bought new potting soil and filled the empty box, and assuming the soil in the second box was fine, she equally distributed a seed packet into the boxes. The seeds in the new rich and fertile soil sprang up quickly. They grew tall and strong with vibrant colors. The seeds in the other box did not fare as well, most growing only to middling height or dying early. It turned out that the soil in that box was rocky and lacked essential nutrients for growth. Jones describes this as "vivid, real-life illustration of the importance of environment."[32] Our schools are the micro-ecosystems of a flower box, and we control the type of soil we offer our students in which to grow. No committed gardener blames the seed for not growing.

The second metaphor is borrowed from Tupac Shakur's reference to young people who emerge in defiance of socially toxic environments as the "roses that grow from concrete."[33] Concrete is one of the worst imaginable surfaces to grow something in: devoid of essential nutrients and frequently contaminated by pollutants. As with Jones's second flower box, growth in such an environment is painful because all of the basic requirements for healthy development (sun, water, nutrient-rich soil) must be hard-won. The ability to control, in a material way, the litany of social stressors that result from growing up in the concrete is nearly impossible for youth. As educators, then, we must find and create cracks in the concrete. The quality of our teaching, along with the resources and networks we connect our students to, are those cracks. They do not create an ideal environment for growth, but they afford some leakage of sunlight, water, and other resources that provide a justification to hope. Teacher-development programs should make it plain that it takes courage to be a gardener in the concrete. It requires a willingness to embrace a painful path, the only one available when we move in solidarity with our students through those jagged cracks in the concrete.

Tupac's metaphor complicates the application of Jones's analogy to schools because our students do not only live in our schools. They also live in other beds of concrete, where they experience chronic exposure to social toxins. The pain that results from this is carried in the bodies of young people and it crosses the threshold of our schools. There is no getting around this principal fact of teaching, and the fewer the resources the young person has to cope with those social stressors, the more intense their pain will be. Schools have virtually no control over the array of social toxins that their students are exposed to in the meta-ecosystem of our society, but schools can control how they respond to them and this gives me, and the children we serve, the audacity to hope.[34]

This pain that our young people carry manifests in our schools in a variety of ways. Sometimes it takes an obvious form like an outpouring of emotion, which might even be directed at me or another student. Usually, the signs are more subtle, manifesting in classic signs of depression (fatigue, sadness, self-deprecation). In these moments when a child can no longer contain the pain they feel, our response has the potential to add to it—or begin the healing process. We may think that if we send the "disobedient"/"disengaged" child out, we have removed the pain from our system. It simply does not work that way. Rather, when we exclude a child, we introduce another social stressor into the micro-ecosystem of our classroom *and* our larger school environment. We rationalize the exclusion by telling ourselves that we have pulled a weed from the garden, allowing for a healthier environment for the other children to grow. This ignores the fact that every student in our school is part of a delicate balance built on interdependency. Wayne Yang, a high school science and math teacher for over seventeen years, and one of the finest educators I have known in my career, put it this way: "All my students are indigenous to my classroom and therefore there are no weeds in my classroom." From this perspective, the decision to remove a child, rather than to heal them, is not only bad for the child, it is destructive to the social ecosystem of the classroom and the school at large.[35]

I have been teaching long enough to know the enormity of this challenge, particularly because these moments almost always happen when I am convinced we are doing something of the utmost importance in the classroom. But then I think to myself, *How did I get to a place where I am prioritizing lesson plans over healing a child in pain?* This not only ignores my most basic sensibilities as a teacher and school leader, it also disregards years of research documenting the importance of caring, self-esteem, trust, and hope as preconditions for positive educational outcomes.[36]

As educators, we also tend to seriously underestimate the impact our response has on the other students in the school. They are watching us when we interact with their peers. When we become frustrated and punish youth who manifest symptoms of righteous rage or social misery, we legitimate doubts among other students about our capacity to meet their needs if they are ever in pain. At the end of the day, effective teaching depends most heavily on one thing—deep and caring relationships, as discussed in great detail in chapter 4. To provide the authentic care that students require from us as a precondition for learning from us, we must connect our indignation over all forms of oppression with a critical hope that we can act to change them.

False hope would have us believe this change will not cost us anything. This kind of false hope is mendacious; it never acknowledges pain. Critical hope stares down the painful path, and despite the overwhelming odds against us making it down that path to change, we make the journey, again and again. There is no other choice. Acceptance of this fact allows us to find the courage and the commitment to cajole our students to join us on that journey. This makes us better people as it makes us better educators, and it models for our students that the painful path *is* the hopeful path.

INTERRUPTING STEREOTYPE THREAT

When students are more hopeful, they are more likely to interrupt what Claude Steele and Joshua Aronson's research coined as *stereotype threat*.[37] If you test students, you should know what stereotype threat is. It is some of the most important research we have to explain why so many students of color, regardless of zip code and parent income, underperform on standardized tests in comparison to many of their white and Asian counterparts.

In short, stereotype threat is triggered in the body when a negative performance stereotype exists about a group with which you identify yourself. The existence of this stereotype, even if one does not personally subscribe to it, naturally triggers elevated levels of anxiety and stress in the body. These elevated levels create a physiological reaction that releases hormones like adrenaline and cortisol in the body to fight off the perceived threat posed by the stress. This biochemical reaction interrupts brain activity and literally diminishes the working memory such that students underperform, even on subject matter they have proven competent in under non-triggering environments.

What Steele and others have found in their research is that the key trigger for a student's stereotype threat is the messaging, explicit or implied, that the test being administered will measure one's innate abilities in the areas where the group stereotype is that the group is not "naturally" good in that area. After the early research on stereotype threat emerged in the mid- to late 1990s, other researchers began exploring the phenomenon in other groups as the validity of the concept rested, at least partially, on proving that it affected other groups under similar conditions.

If stereotype threat were real, then surely the effects would show up for women too. So Steven Spencer sought to test the impact of stereotype threat on women on performance-related tasks in math. The strong hold that patriarchy continues to have on our society's consciousness has resulted in a sensibility that women are less natu-rally inclined to succeed in fields related to math and science. The story is never that women *cannot* find success in those fields, only that they are not innately wired to thrive in math and science and so they will just have to work extra hard to develop the skills that men have "more naturally." As part of his research, Spencer studied a group of women mathematicians, which means—well, they can do math.[38] When presented with a problem set well within their math-ematical skill level and told that the test would measure their innate mathematical ability, the women notably underperformed.

Perhaps the last frontier for convincing the research commu-nity that stereotype needed to be taken seriously was proving that it also impacted white men. The stereotype that researchers took on for white men is the belief that white men are not naturally gifted athletically. In 1999, Jeff Stone's research did just that.[39] Stone and his research partners selected a group of white male athletes and put them through an athletic test that they were told would measure their "natural athletic ability" and they notably underperformed in relationship to the control group.

Since the late 1990s, numerous studies have continued to ex-plore and examine the impact of stereotype effect on various groups. It is now widely accepted in the field of psychology as a phenomenon that affects all groups of people. However, the stereotypes that affect white men are not life-threatening, but stereotypes affecting Black, Latinx, Indigenous, Pacific Islander, and Southeast Asian youth are, and this is why curriculum and pedagogy that affirms our youth and their cultural identities is so important. When curriculum and peda-gogy consistently illuminate the genius of these cultural groups and their histories, while also critically interrogating the various histori-cal causes of the inequities they experience, young people are better equipped to interrupt stereotype threat.

The research also clearly reveals that the messaging that educators use to shape the importance of an exam can diminish the effect of stereotype threat. In other words, we have to be explicit with students about what tests do, and do not, measure. If we know the stereotype is that youth of color and youth in poverty do not typically perform well on exams, then those youth certainly also know that stereotype. This means it is highly likely that when they sit for the exam, their anxiety levels will jack up and their physiology will respond accordingly. We also know that we can mitigate some of those negative reactions by explicitly telling students that the test is a problem-solving task that says nothing about ability.

REVEALING THE PYGMALION EFFECT

In their 1968 groundbreaking study, where they coined the term *Pygmalion effect*, Rosenthal and Jacobson revealed what we have long suspected about the relationship between teacher expectations and student performance.[40] In what came to be known as the "Oak School experiment," Rosenthal and Jacobson wanted to know what would happen if a group of elementary school teachers believed particular students were capable of academic "blooming" or "spurting," even if their test scores did not suggest that likelihood. They appropriated Flanagan's Tests of General Ability (TOGA) and turned it into a fictitious test that they called the "Harvard Test of Inflected Acquisition," which purported to measure a student's likelihood to intellectually bloom. Teachers at the Oak School administered the tests, but it was the research team that evaluated them. Then, using a process of random selection, the research team gave teachers a class list to start the next school year that identified a percentage of their new class as "spurters," suggesting that if the teachers could create the proper environment, then these children were well positioned to show strong academic gains.

The study tracked the growth of these "special" students against their classmates and found that, indeed, the elevated teacher expectation created a noticeable effect on student achievement. The effect was particularly pronounced in the younger grades, but it also showed up with older students. In their retrospective, the authors wrote, "[I]t's been a long time since the original Pygmalion experiment showed a significant effect of teacher expectations on pupils' intellectual development. Along the way there have been a lot of studies in laboratories and in schools to show that expectancy effects occur and there have been a lot of studies to investigate how they occur. . . . Most of what we really wanted to know is, unfortunately, still not known."[41]

In the three decades that have passed since they wrote that retrospective, we have gained tremendous insight into why teacher expectation matters so much for student engagement and achievement. What Rosenthal and Jacobson began to reveal for us is some of the essence of the psychology of teacher expectation, much of which comes back to the research discussed in the chapter 4 about relationships. Research on unconscious bias has exploded in the last decade, revealing that the various racial and social biases that have been coded into each teacher's psyche form powerful expectations for behavior, engagement, and ability.[42] These manifest as perceptions and expectations about a student's capacity to learn, and when they are left unchecked and buried in the unconscious, it is much more likely that a teacher will rationalize student failure as reflective of the student's lack of ability rather than as a circumstance of the teacher's pedagogy. We saw this shift in the Oak School experiment because those teachers believed certain students were "special." When those students struggled, it became much more difficult to blame the student; for if the "special" student is failing, who is actually failing? The real power of teacher expectation rests in the will and skill of the teacher to modify their pedagogical practice to be responsive to a student's needs (social, physical, emotional, spiritual, and intellectual). For several decades now, we have referred to this as "differentiated instruction," the gold standard of high-quality teaching.[43] In truth though, a teacher's commitment to lovingly draw out the potential of every student lies at the heart of the pedagogy of the best educators throughout the history of our time-honored craft.

FOSTERING A CRITICAL GROWTH MINDSET

If we follow this logic pattern of the impact of relevance on young people to its conclusion, we end up with an environment that cultivates what Carol Dweck has called a "growth mindset."[44] If you have worked in schools within the last decade, especially in schools serving children of color and children in poverty, you have surely been encouraged to use Dweck's work. Her work has come to feel like a mandatory pairing with Angela Duckworth's *Grit* in schools all over the country.[45]

I am deeply concerned with the ways that both of these concepts have found their ways into schools, not because I am a non-believer in the importance of mindset and grit, but because both approaches seem to have failed to grasp the ways that an overwhelmingly white teaching force would use these ideas to justify their own failures with children. What I have watched unfold in school after school that has attempted to implement these concepts as key pedagogical strategies for increasing test scores is that grit and growth mindset become a salve for the wounded egos of educators who continually fail to create successful classroom environments for vulnerable children.[46] Teachers and school leaders who truly believe that all children are capable know that struggles in their classroom and school are about their classroom and school, not about the absence of grit and growth mindsets in children. They know that, by definition, the most wounded children have bucketloads of grit and a willingness to try new strategies and work hard. They tap the deep reservoirs of resilience that Tupac Shakur describes as the "damaged petals" that reveal the "tenacity and will to reach the sun" in every rose that grows in the concrete.[47]

It has been my recurring experience that far too many teachers in schools that have adopted grit and growth mindset as focal strategies for teaching are able to locate the problem in the child. Dweck started to acknowledge this issue nearly ten years after her book was released, writing that:

> I fear that the mindset work is sometimes used to justify why some students aren't learning: "Oh, he has a fixed mindset." We used [growth mindset] to blame the child's environment or ability. Must it always come back to finding a reason why some children just can't learn, as opposed to finding a way to help them learn? Teachers who understand the growth mindset do everything in their power to unlock that learning.[48]

While doing work with educators in Australia, Dweck's colleague Susan Mackie identified these misapplications of Dweck's work as "false growth mindset."[49] What Dweck and Mackie now bang their drums about is the fact that a student's mindset tends to reflect the educator's mindset. So, if a student has a fixed mindset in your class, then that probably means that you have a fixed mindset toward that child. If we want children to believe that they can grow their minds, then we must model that by growing our minds about the ways in which we teach them. The same can be said for grit. It is generally not our young people who lack the grit to learn, but adults who lack the grit to change how we structure and support learning in our schools.

At the end of day, the development pattern laid out in this chapter is consistent for children who are involved with educational experiences that are relevant to them, and this results in a revealing of their already well-developed growth mindsets. I have referred to this as a "critical growth mindset" to emphasize that this growth mindset we want to see in children gets activated only when the curriculum and pedagogy are relevant to the material conditions of the child. To create relevance in the form of community-responsive pedagogy demands that we are self-critical when the lessons and approaches we design do not land well with our students.

CLOSING THE KNOWING-DOING GAP: WHAT DOES RELEVANCE LOOK LIKE IN PRACTICE?

Te Whānau o Tupuranga: When an Entire Institution Commits to Relevance

I have been in classrooms and schools all over the world, and there is no school that does relevance better than Te Whānau o Tupuranga, the Māori school within Kia Aroha College, a year 7–10 (grades 6–12) high school in New Zealand. The other two "schools" within the college prioritize Samoan and Tongan languages and cultures. I have spent weeks at a time embraced by, and embedded in, the school and community on numerous occasions over the past twenty years. On my very first visit there, and on every visit since, I have been witness to some of the finest evidence I have seen about the positive impacts on children and families in a school that understands that relevance requires emphasizing knowledge over information. Knowledge is a gift. Knowledge is the gift of your ancestors. Knowledge is the gift of your history. Knowledge is the gift of understanding your own value. Knowledge is the gift of a deeper awareness about your sacred purpose on this planet. I am not saying that schools should not be giving out information. Information has its role, but it has gotten out of its place. We have hyper-invested in the distribution and regurgitation of information at the expense of knowledge.

Let us look at this distinction more personally. Think about the last time you gave a gift to someone. After you gave that gift, did you return a few days later and tell the recipient that the following week you would be back again to administer a timed examination to determine the degree to which they have properly received and interpreted the gift you gave them? I truly hope you did not, because that would be utterly absurd, and quite weird.

This is how we know that the primary purpose of schools currently serving vulnerable children is the dissemination of information and not the gifting of knowledge. The majority, and sometimes the entirety, of the school day and school year centers around the transference, regurgitation, and assessment of information. I am not necessarily against testing children for their understanding of information we are imparting to them, but we have gone way too far with this investment and at the expense of teaching children the deeper, more lasting, and more valuable cultural knowledge that is medicine for their mind, body, emotion, and spirit.

Tupuranga is commited to prioritizing Māori cultural knowledge. It is the only school I have seen where the institutional identity is focused on the "transformative health and healing philosophy" of "la cultura cura." *La cultura cura* literally translates to "the culture cures." But, as is often the case, much is lost in that translation. What it really means is that your culture is your medicine. I was first introduced to this concept by the National Compadres Network (NCN) and have spent the better part of my time as an educator trying to cultivate spaces that make it foundational. The NCN describes this approach to teaching as lifting ourselves and our children up by our "rootstraps."

No school institution that I have witnessed better embodies this philosophy than Kia Aroha, where they tell children, "First, you are Māori. And until you understand that fact and what that means, anything else that I might try to teach you is a waste of time." They want children to read, do algebra, experiment in chemistry—but they want them to do those things as Māori. If they do not, then they will read through someone else's lens, which means they will not really be *reading*. They might learn the mechanics of reading, writing, and math, but to learn these things through the lens of others is never to actually *become* a reader, a writer, or a mathematician—at least not in the deeper and more transformative sense of those identities. You must read and interpret through the lens of your ancestors and your culture. Then, and only then, will you truly understand what you are reading because you will understand it as Māori.

What happens at Tupuranga, because they give their young people the gift of knowledge, is that that gift sits with the children and they get to choose when, where, how, and with whom they share what their school has taught them. In my time with the Māori, other Pacific Indigenous peoples, Indigenous peoples in this country, and my own Indigenous teachers and elders, the practice of mixing medicines has been engrained in my understanding of what it means to be culturally and community relevant. If we believe that our culture is our medicine and we deny children their birthright to bring their medicine with them into our schools, then we are by definition making them sick.

The culture of schools is also medicine. But if a child's experience is regularly such that they are not permitted to share their medicine and are at the same time having the medicine of the school shoved down their throats, it is hard to imagine them feeling well. In a place like Tupuranga, the culture of the school centralizes and insists that children bring forth their culture as an inseparable element of their intellectual development. Curriculum and assessment are designed to ensure a mixing of medicines, where students learn reading, writing, and arithmetic with the expressed intent of understanding their responsibility to themselves, their ancestors, their families, and their community to transform their learning into community actualization and cultural perpetuity.

On the last day of my first visit to Tupuranga, I experienced one of the finest forms of evidence about how this emphasis on knowledge over information transforms the lives of young people. We were in our final hour at the school before we were to head out to the Auckland airport. As is Māori cultural custom, the school community performed *poroporoaki*, a farewell ceremony to bless our journey home. All of the students and staff gathered in the school's multipurpose room, and we stood in front of them to receive the ceremonial medicine they prepared for us in the form of a traditional song and *haka*. In their Indigenous language, a language that the majority of the students had lost prior to attending Tupuranga, the students performed a *waiata* (song) called "Te Aniwaniwa," which describes the beauty around us and looking for all things positive. Then the whole school performed a *haka* called "Huakina. Huakina," that was written to unite schools going to the Secondary Kapa Haka (Māori Performing Arts) National Competitions and now is performed to unite voices from Auckland with others. So, using it for us was a song of solidarity that includes words such as: "Let our ancestors be with us from the North, West, South and East, so that we reach all the corners of Mother Earth."

The student performance was one of the most powerful displays of meaningful learning I have witnessed in any school. But what happened next brought me to tears. Immediately following the coordinated and beautifully choreographed performance of the *waiata* and *haka*, every member of the school community lined up for *hariru*, which is literally "to shake hands." But different from so many other cultures, for the Māori the concept is that now that we have challenged and checked that you are prepared to come in peace and be friends of ours, we will share the same breath in the *hongi* (touching of our noses and taking a deep breath together) and we become all one *whānau* (family).

After a couple of minutes working through the line of young people and staff members, something unexpected took place that none of the staff knew had been planned. Each day that I visited the school during my two weeks, I met with a group of students and we shared *palabra* (the word) and we mixed our medicines. A group of about fifteen boys who were frequently part of those medicine moments decided to give me a gift that in Māori culture you cannot ask for. Only Māori can decide who is deserving of this gift. These boys would likely not have had this gift to give me if it were not for Tupuranga's commitment to cultural and community relevance. Nor would the space have been available in a school environment for those boys to honor me in that way. The *hariru* stopped. The air went out of the room. These fifteen boys performed a *haka* called "Tika Tonu" to honor our relationship and the medicine that we had shared. According to Ann Milne, who was the long-standing principal of the school at the time:

> This is a very well-known haka, written in 1914 by a chief for his son, who was at a white boarding school and getting into difficulty. The *haka* title means "What is right is always right." The message of the *haka* is of challenge, struggle, perseverance, and achievement. It's performed on many different occasions. It tells young people the message the writer gave to his son in the lyrics, to know who they are—"So son, although it may be difficult for you, and son, although it seems to be unyielding no matter how long you reflect on it, the answer to the problem is here inside you."[50]

The entire school community circled in behind and around the boys to support the ceremonial medicine they had decided to pour into me in those last few moments I had with them. Even now, as I retell this story, I can feel the emotion welling up in me. I stood facing them with tears streaming down my face, never more aware of the power and import of self-determination in the education of our children.

So many of the children who are struggling in our schools come from warrior cultures. Our national response to their struggles has been to build schools that tell children to "work hard and be nice." When that young person's warrior culture begins to emerge, we punish it, we grind it out of them, instead of seeing that as the teachings of their ancestors emerging as a way to illuminate their path to self-esteem, freedom, and sacredness. Schools would do well to learn from Tupuranga how to embrace that as a pathway to rigor, justice, and democracy instead of trying to physically control it and silence it.

In all my years working with Tupuranga, I had never seen the test score data that they reported to their national ministry of education. Frankly, I never thought to ask because I consistently witnessed the real-time data of students performing what they had learned, and the rigor needed to produce that data was undeniable to me. However, in 2015 Ann Milne came to Oakland, California, to keynote a conference we were hosting on community-responsive pedagogy. In her presentation, she showed their data in the form of a change over time graph (see figure 5.2) that is the most compelling educational data I have ever seen.

In New Zealand, they were measuring school performance based on the "NZ National Standards" by tracking reading, writing, and math scores on nationally standardized benchmarks. As a public school, Tupuranga is expected to adhere to these measurements of student progress. However, Tupuranga has also chosen to measure

<<AU: Is amended title OK?>>

FIGURE 5.2 Tupuranga's leading and lagging indicators

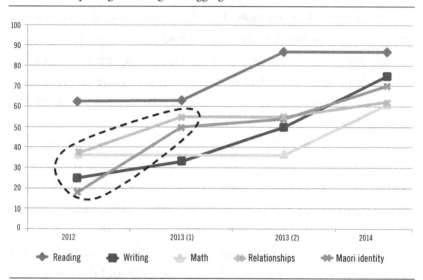

Source: Ann Milne, presentation given at the Teaching Excellence Network Annual Conference, gave in Oakland, California, in 2015.
Note: Maori identity is the school's internal measurement scale.

relationships and cultural identity[51]—the things that neuroscience, child development, and psychology all agree are core preconditions necessary for improving reading, writing, and math scores. But we do not measure these things because they do not matter all that much in our schools. They matter so little in our school contexts because the children whom our society believes matter come to school with those things largely intact and secured by all of our major institutions. So, why measure it? Tupuranga knows better for Māori youth.

What is also compelling about Tupuranga's data is that it is longitudinal. So many of the schools that claim to be data driven are looking at snapshot data and making knee-jerk decisions based on that moment-in-time data. In the case of Tupuranga, they are looking at data over time. They are also triangulating their data by drawing from multiple data sources. They are looking at process data to understand their outcome data. They are methodologically rigorous with how they use data because they are less concerned with being data driven and more concerned with being driven by the right data.

Attention to data that is informing us about the well-being of children, the clearly established preconditions for consistent engagement and learning, *is* the right data. Tupuranga might well be considered a continuation school in the US context. The school serves middle school- and high school–aged youth, some of whom have come to Tupuranga after struggling in mainstream white New Zealand schools. Given the negative school histories of so many of their students, it is not shocking that in the aggregate students do not score out all that well on cultural identity and relationships when they first arrive at Tupuranga. Their test scores look very similar to those of Black, Latinx, Indigenous, Pacific Islander, and other non-dominant youth in the US context. All these children live in a society that teaches them to hate themselves—to hate the color of their skin, the texture of their hair, their eye color, the language they speak, the neighborhoods they come from, and their ancestors. Sometimes that teaching is implicit. Sometimes that teaching is explicit. But it is taught by this nation all the time, and New Zealand is not all that different in that regard. And because we do not measure these things, we do not actually know how our children are doing on these foundational developmental factors, even though all of the research is telling us that these factors are essential for a strong and healthy identity, and by extension, success in school and in life.

Educators at Tupuranga do know how their children are doing on these essential factors because they measure it. And so what we see over the course of year 1 in Tupuranga's data is significant growth in cultural identity and relationships because that is what the school focuses on: "First, you are Māori. You must understand your language. You must understand your culture." There is tremendous academic rigor there. But, reading, writing, and math scores are all flat in that first year. In the US context, when we see this snapshot, we bail and use arguments that we cannot justify Ethnic Studies because it does not help students learn to read and write better, it just makes them angry.

So why doesn't Tupuranga bail? Because it is Māori, that's why. When a Māori educator at Tupuranga looks at a Māori child who is not reading, writing, or doing math well, their response is different. Their reaction is "Oh . . . you don't even know who you are yet, so of course you are not doing reading, writing, and math. You don't know that I cannot teach you reading, writing, and math. That knowledge is actually your birthright. I can't teach that to you, I can only help pull it out of you. And if it's not coming out of you yet, it's because you don't know who you are." These educators double down on cultural identity and relationships, and over time the other measures of learning begin to take shape.

Anyone who has closely read the research in neuroscience, physiology, psychology, social epidemiology, and child development knows precisely why this happens in this way. The simplest way to explain it is to think of those precondition factors (self-esteem, love and belonging, etc.) as one end of a tether. On the other end of that tether sit test scores and other measures of academic success established by the dominant culture. This is why the Tupuranga data graph is such a powerful visual of what the research is telling us. Those precondition elements are the pull agents in the tethered relationship. They are the leading indicators of student growth. Test scores and the like are the pulled agents in the tether. They are the lag indicators. So, because children are coming to school with the core drivers of achievement under full assault, the drivers of change in the tether are sitting slack below the very indicators that they are meant to be pulling up. The data graph beautifully displays the commonsense expectation that all that slack has to be taken up, the lead indicators have to get above the lag indicators before they can start pulling them upward. The lesson of Tupuranga is that when you change the data you look at, it changes the questions you ask. And when you change the questions you ask, you start coming up with different answers. Tupuranga chose to measure what matters in the school, and as a result the children actually feel and perform like they matter.

No school that I have visited has ever had a greater impact on my life, my research, my teaching, my family, and my understanding of our culture being our medicine than Te Whānau o Tupuranga in Otara, New Zealand. I returned to Oakland all those years ago changed forever. Seeing is believing, and for the first time in my life, I had seen what was possible in schools when we decide that the primary purpose of schools is the wellness of the children who walk through the doors every day. Just a few years later, with the wind of our Māori ukukura beneath our wings, we endeavored to open the Roses in Concrete Community School in East Oakland, California, modeled after many of the things the Māori have taught us over the years.[52] That school, those boys, those teachers, that community changed me and, as a result, they changed my community by reminding us it is our birthright to give our children the gift of knowledge of self that we might be self-determining, community actualized, and live in cultural perpetuity.

In both of these examples, Tupuranga and the Tucson example discussed below, the work of creating a relevant curriculum and pedagogy was about connecting young people to a purpose and identity bigger than themselves. This is what Maslow did not get. A young person cannot be well if they are thriving in school and life while others around them are suffering. The same is true for us as adults. Inequality and inequity will undo all of us. The sooner we figure that out, the sooner we will find the courage to make fundamental changes in how schools operate in our society. The sooner that happens, the sooner we will start growing generations of young people prepared to meet the challenge and moral obligation of building a just and sustainable democracy.

Augustine Romero: Reflections on Tucson's MARS Program

I have seen practices that were similarly effective as those I have discussed at Kia Aroha in the United States. But the only time I have seen them is either in individual classrooms or programs, never across an entire school and certainly never across an entire school system. The closest that I have been to seeing community-responsive practices implemented across a school system was in the work of the Mexican American/Raza Studies (MARS) program in Tucson, Arizona. The program was so politically and pedagogically powerful for students and families, and also disruptive to the dominant narrative, that it came under constant attack from conservative interests in the state. In 2010, the Arizona House of Representatives passed House Bill 2281, deeming the purpose of the program, its curriculum, and its pedagogy as seditious. Although the ruling was overturned some seven years later by the 9th Circuit Federal Court of Appeals, the damage was done. Despite multiple efforts by community, teachers, and students, the program was effectively gutted and thus many of its proponents now do work outside the state to try to support the development of similar efforts around the country.

One of those closest to the birth and design of the program was one of its architects, Augustine "Auggie" Romero. There is so much learning that we can gain from educators who have blazed paths in classrooms and programs that should inform how we move this work forward. As with any effort so ambitious and committed to deep transformation, there were missteps and painful mistakes that we must include in our calculus as we continue to push forward on efforts to normalize equity and community-responsive pedagogy in our schools. What follows is an interview I did with Auggie to try to capture some of that learning from his community's journey to create an educational experience for children that was truly relevant to their historical and lived experiences.

JDA: *Can you share a bit about your ancestral and personal history and how that brought you into working with young people?*

AR: Yes, I'm a quarter Yaqui. My mom's dad was full Yaqui. My Nana on my mom's side was from the Pima people. They're relatives of the Tohono O'odham. They're basically cousins. They might be considered O'odham, but they call themselves Pima. On my dad's side, we know they're Yaqui as well, but they're not registered. And of course, like people in this part of the world on my dad's side of the family, are part Apache. I'm sure there's some Spanish too.

And just in terms of knowing who I am and where I come from was always really powerful. My dad was real heavy into who we were and would tell stories about those things. And I was always intrigued by those stories, and then listening to my grandfather on my dad's side tell stories about his ancestors was always interesting to me. We would often be out hunting or fishing, and like a movie, we'd be sitting around the campfire telling stories. I never got tired of those stories.

Fast-forward about fifteen years later, and I decided to become an educator. When I graduated from Tucson High School, I remember looking at the main building of the school and thinking, "I'm never, ever coming back here again." I mean, I hated my educational experience. I hated it. I was blessed in the sense that I had about an ounce of baseball talent. And that got me a baseball scholarship, or a couple of different baseball scholarships, along the way. Had it not been for baseball, I'm not sure I would've gotten my bachelor's degree. After my undergraduate studies, particular areas such as Marxist theory and Chicano Studies, captured my interest, and I started to wonder about and understand why I hated my educational experience so much.

So, I came home to Tucson after college and I became a coach and I was pretty good at it. As a coach, I just naturally did more than just coach. I was teaching, mentoring, connecting to kids' lives, trying to get to know them in a more real and deeper manner, trying to connect to them on an authentic level. That was a powerful experience for me. At the same time, I was preparing to go to law school. I applied to nine different law schools and got into five, and I was on my way.

In the summer of 1994, I went to Alaska to make money to pay for law school. Before I left for Alaska, I went with my brother-in-law to the College of Education at the University of Arizona. And back in the day, the application for the post-baccalaureate program was literally two pieces of paper. And you sat there at a desk or a table, and you filled out the application—pen and paper—and then you submitted it. And that's literally what I did. About two weeks before I came home from Alaska, I called home, and my mom said I had this huge packet from the College of Education. So, I asked her to open it. And she said, "You've been accepted to some post-baccalaureate program." So, it was that point in time where I made two decisions about my life. I was going to come home and ask my then partner, Eydie, to marry me. And I was going to become an educator.

JDA: *Wow. I don't think I ever heard that story before.*

AR: Wait—let me tell you the next part. Then, I had to tell my dad I wasn't going to be a lawyer. And ever since I was little, he had been saying that I was going to be his lawyer. He had this fascination about law. So, when I came home, I asked him if I could meet with him at his house and get his blessing on two things. And he says, of course. Once we got to my dad's house, he said "What are these blessings you are seeking?" I said, "I want to ask Eydie to marry me. I need your blessing." And he's like, "Of course, of course." He was real happy about it. For my dad, Eydie was like the daughter he never had. Then later on, my dad says, "Mijo, what was the other thing?" I thought that for sure he's going to forget about it. And I was going to let the day slide and ask another day. But he asked, so I told him I wasn't going to go to law school and that I was going to be a teacher. And he says, "Ay, Mijo, don't do that because you're going to be poor your whole life."

I told him that it was what I wanted, and so he gave his blessing. That was the summer of 1994. Six years later, in March of 2000, and we are on the third floor of St. Mary's Hospital and my dad is quite literally on his deathbed. Now, mind you, I thought I'd let him down by not becoming a lawyer. And I'm sitting there in the hospital with him, and he puts his hand in my hand and he says, "Mijo, did I ever tell you how proud I am that you became a teacher?" And I said, "Dad, all these years I thought I'd let you down." And he said "Mijo, do you know what the apostles called Jesus? They called him teacher, son. And that's your responsibility to this world."

Two days later, my dad was gone. You know, this work is so spiritual. And for me, that's where it comes from. It's spiritual work. That inner self, that inner sense of doing and serving and being, and that's where it all came from for me.

JDA: *Wow. That's a beautiful story. Thank you for sharing that. So, fast-forward to present day. What is the work that you're currently engaged in, and what are your hopes for how it might impact non-dominant communities generally and young people specifically?*

AR: I started consulting with something I call "We Schools." I framed it after the song that one of our students brought to our class called "They Schools" by Dead Prez. If you listen to the lyrics of that song, they really break down schools in terms that reflect how many of students have felt along the way. They felt the same way in terms of how education was basically trying to domesticate them, not trying to enlighten them, not trying to have them recognize and understand their true capacities as thinkers, as intellectuals, and as human beings.

We Schools is an attempt to further the work we started in Tucson all those years ago and trying to create schools where students develop a strong sense of identity, purpose, and hope. We use an equity framework and try to push that agenda based on the education, all the different lessons I received from our students over the course of the nearly ten and a half years of doing this work in Tucson Unified. They taught us so many things about how hard and how important it to involve ourselves in an intellectual project that uses education as a tool towards deeper levels of humanization, liberation, and intellectualism.

JDA: *Can you describe a little bit about how the program that gave you all these lessons from students came about?*

AR: Well, the Mexican American/Raza Studies Program (MARS) came to fruition in July of 1997. And there was the strongest push coming from a community group called CONMAS (community, organizations and neighborhoods for Mexican American Studies). For the first few years, they laid some of the groundwork. In 2002, TUSD started looking for a new director for the program. At the time, I was teaching high school and the deputy superintendent came to my classroom and pulled me out. And, we quite literally went across the hall into a broom closet. It was sort of our teacher's lounge, but it was more like a broom closet. And I'm not exaggerating when I say she quizzed me for like three hours and asked me every question under the sun about curriculum, about pedagogy, about students, about parents, about community engagement. In the course of that conversation, I got a little spiritual on her because I knew that she was raised Catholic like me. We even used to go to the same church, and she would always sit a couple of rows in front of me. And so here she is asking me about creating a program that would alleviate the achievement gap for Latinos. And I basically told her, "What I can do for you is what I do in my classroom."

And she asked, "What's that?"

And I asked her if she was familiar with the temptation of Christ? And she says, "Yes." And I said, "So tell me why is it that Satan could not tempt Christ?" And you know, she gave me answers like, "Oh, because he was son of God, blah, blah, blah."

And I said, "Well, he was the son of God. But most important was that he knew who he was. He knew he was son of God. He had a clear identity . . . he knew who he was." And then I told her that what I try to do in the classroom is to help our students gain a deeper understanding of who they are, where they come from, what they are about. This is the idea of purpose and that their purpose in the world was to transform themselves, their environments, and their communities.

And then I told her that, like Jesus, our students are the hope of the world. This group of kids that are in my classroom right now, they're the hope of the world. And then that's how I got involved. That conversation was in April of 2002. In June of 2002, I was confirmed as the acting director.

JDA: *So, you have written about this, but how would you describe the pedagogical framework that guided the program? And specifically, I'm asking how did you do what you did, and why were you choosing those things as your guiding framework?*

AR: The framework came to be known as critically compassionate intellectualism (CCI). This was back in the day, when critical pedagogies were fighting with critical race theorists. People were fighting for space. So, let me back up. In August of 2004, we had seventeen kids in the class. The same seventeen kids that started with us in May of 2003.

And every one of them had dropped out at some point before that. One girl was a four-time dropout. Another was a two-time dropout. Anyway, it was the end of the year, and I walked into the class of one of our teachers and I asked him if I could ask the students a question. He said, "Go for it, Bro. Go for it." So, I looked at the whole class and I asked them, "Why are you all still here?"

And what they said over and over again was that it came down to what we were teaching them and how we were teaching them—the curriculum and the pedagogy. The curriculum piece was about the fact that we were teaching them about themselves, teaching them about their ancestors. But how we did that was important. Going back to that Dead Prez example because there were other people on this cultural piece wanting to go back to the ancestors, but it didn't have the same effect as our approach. What I try to impress upon people is that it cannot just be about the ancestors. Our focus was on: "Who are you? Where are you? What are you trying to become?" Then when they would answer those questions, we would move to: "Where do those answers come from? Who put those answers in your head? Why did they give you those answers? Why are those answers so important?"

For us and for the students, the opportunity to pose and answer those questions as a normal part of the school day was profound. They did the work because they wanted to answer those questions. They wanted to think about those things. Like Dead Prez says, "Tell me how to get drugs out of my barrio; tell me how to prevent my dad from beating my mom." Like that. That's what kids wanted to know and understand. So, we talked about identity. It isn't even about who they were "racially" or "culturally" yet. It started with [an "I am poem"], who are you as YaYa, as Sally, as Stephanie, as Jorge . . . Who are you? Why are you this person? What are your fears? What are your desires? What are your hopes? What are your dreams? People trivialize this part of the work, but over the course of the two years we were together, our kids did that "I Am" poem six different times. Six. And through returning to that assignment periodically, they got more and more clear that these are my fears, these are my desires, these are my dreams, this is what's getting in the way, and this is what I need to do to transform this reality. That's the curriculum they wanted. That's what engaged, empowered, and activated our students.

And alongside of this was the pedagogical piece; how we went about it in terms of our methods of teaching. Core to these methods was the idea that we were in a relationship with each other where we were all both teacher and student simultaneously. I'm learning from you equally, just as you're learning from me. The focus of the pedagogy was really on making sure they felt true empowerment, a real sense of their agency. I remember one day, one of students come to me and he says, "Romero, what do I write, Bro?"

And I said, "Mijo, just tell me what you think."

"Oh, okay, cool," and he walks away. Then he comes back a few minutes later and says, "But, what should I write?"

I said, "You write what you want to write."

He had been so conditioned to people telling him what to write that when we were asking him to tell me what he really thought it created a block for him. "Tell me what you think" didn't register with him. He really struggled in the beginning, as many of our students did, because he was searching for his voice in the school space. His evolution was amazing. He became an outstanding student among outstanding students; one of the deepest thinkers—a true intellectual—in the cohort.

The last piece of this whole discussion about what we did and how we did it was the student-parent-teacher interaction component. I cannot tell you how many students came back to us and said that one of the biggest factors was how we treated them and their parents. Quite literally, it was the fact that they felt we loved, respected, and appreciated them and their families, and their parents felt the same way. One of the more powerful elements of developing these relationships between us, the students, and their families was the "Se-Ollin Parent Encuentros," which we referred to as the representation of blossoming intellectuals. This was an event where students presented their work, their research, to their parents. Parents would trip out. They would be like, "Did you just call my daughter an intellectual?" And I'm like, "Yeah, I did. Go over there and ask her what she's doing. I'll bet you she wants to sit there with you and explain what's going on." Or we would have parents come to the Encuentros and say, "I had to come see what you're doing because I can't get her to shut up about this stuff."

So, parents were like, "What's going on? Why do you suddenly want to go to school?" You know, we had daughters and sons pulling their parents to these events. The same kids that did not want their parents to attend parent-teacher conferences and open houses were now making their parents come to our Encuentros.

JDA: *Can you talk a little bit about the role that relationships and your responsibility played in that approach?*

AR: We saw our students as humans and our students saw us as human beings who were just like them. They wanted to see us lead. They really, really wanted to see us lead. And in that way of leading that I have been describing, it gave them examples of how they could come back and lead as well. And when we screwed up—and we did lots of times, and sometimes big-time screw ups—this also gave them examples of how *not* to lead.

I remember the first time we did the "I Am" poems. And myself and another teacher got up there first and we rocked our own "I Am" poems. We had done the assignment just like students. This was part of us seeing each other as human beings so that they knew that telling all of our stories was important to the work we were doing together. This was not just an assignment given from teacher to student. This was an assignment for our community, our Social Justice Education Project community, our classroom community. After we performed our poems, a whole bunch of the kids, were like "Oh, hell no." They weren't shying away from it. They saw how we turned it up and how we represented, and they asked for more time so that they could redo their poems because they had seen more of what was possible if they approached the work with their souls and hearts. Before that, they had the sort of standard poems; things like "My dream is to become a major league baseball player, blah, blah, blah." Not that that dream is bad at all, but, you know, it was very basic and barely scratching the surface of who they were. So, we honored their request and we changed the schedule to give them more time. And they honored us and themselves and they rocked it.

When we came back the following year and that cohort was all seniors and the next cohort was in the program. And like I said, we did the "I Am" poems again, and they didn't go as well. And we were trying to figure out what happened. We were debriefing with the students and one of our students says, "You know what happened? You guys didn't go up there this year. When you guys went up there, you opened up your hearts. You opened your hearts to me [*gesturing the pulling open of the chest to reveals the heart*] and people could see inside. Once you opened that up and people could see inside, they knew that you were for real, that's when they came, and they wanted to get real. But until that time they were still guarded. But when you went down like that, we took our armor off and said, 'Okay, cool, in this class you can hit it. Here we come. Now we're going to come real.'"

So, we took her lead on that and sure enough, every time after that we would present our poems, and each time the student performances were amazing. Students want to be recognized for their full intellectual capacities. They want to be honored. They want to be respected. And part of that means that we need to reveal ourselves to them. They need to know that they can trust us. They needed to know that what we were asking them to do isn't anything that we wouldn't do ourselves.

You know, I was looking at the literature and what people have been saying about relevance and whatnot. And where I tried to live was inside this idea of being responsive. When folks talk about relevance, they are usually talking about curriculum. And that's fine. I'm not knocking that at all. But I want that curriculum to be responsive to the students' lives. So, how am I responsive to their academic needs? How am I responsive to their social needs? How am I responsive to their teenage needs? You know . . . How are we real? Because to be relevant is almost like I'm going to do something that *matches*. Versus when I think about responsive, I'm going to do something that's *meaningful*. You're going to *feel* it. You know, it's like you're here and you're crying and you're telling me what you need. Now I got to go look for different intersections, different places, different spaces, different people I can go to, to get you what you need. That's *not* relevant. That's responsive. That was the deeper place we tried to get to.

Not all teachers are going to believe in foundational element of responsiveness. All I know is that when teachers didn't believe in it, they didn't believe in our kids, and those teachers didn't have the same level of success as our other teachers because they couldn't get our students to that place wherein our student realized their true intellectual and humanistic capacities.

JDA: *Can you give me an example of this kind of responsiveness with a student?*

AR: Yeah. We had this student; I'll call him JD. He was involved in some—you know, he went sideways. He was shoplifting and allegedly a cop got hit. So, now he's in jail and he gets out, but he doesn't call us when he's in jail. But he comes to us two days later because he's got to go to court and he needs help. And his parents ain't got no money and he's going to get a public defender. And you know what usually happens if you get a public defender. So, we call our friend at the Pima County Defender's office. Our friend gets our student set up with this badass attorney. In the end, JD was there, but he didn't punch the cop. He didn't even steal. He was just there. As a result, he gets off with community service. Had we not been there, he probably gets wrapped up with the other homie and is down for some time. That was all about relationships and our responsibility to building and sustaining those relationships.

REALITY CHECK

The banning of the Ethnic Studies program in Tucson is criminal. However, the greater crime lies in the fact that we still need Ethnic Studies programs. It suggests that we have made virtually no progress in the fifty years since the student strikes at San Francisco State University that fought for classes that taught the history of people of color. Indeed, the case in Arizona suggests that we are going backward in our commitment to serving students of color in our public schools. Given that schools are a social mirror, this reflects poorly on our society's commitment to becoming the multiracial, pluralistic democracy it has promised to become and that it touts itself as all around the world.

In a society that is as racially and ethnically diverse as ours, there is simply no reason that every course that students take should be anything less than an Ethnic Studies course. Let me also point out that people of various European descents have ethnic cultures and many of those cultures are taught matter-of-factly, every day in schools as a normal part of the curriculum—they don't call it Ethnic Studies, but it is. The fact that students and families whose origins fall outside of Europe are forced to ask for separate courses so that they can learn about their ancestors and the ways in which they have shaped the history of the United States and the world is absurd—it's also racist. The need for Ethnic Studies courses puts us in a legal time warp, running us all the way back to the Supreme Court's 1896 *Plessy v. Ferguson* decision that separate and equal was acceptable.[53]

As a nation, we cannot even meet a pathetically low social standard from the nineteenth century. Instead, every day in schools and communities all over this nation, we maintain a de facto position of separate and unequal. Despite the Supreme Court's 1954 promise of "all deliberate speed" to create racially integrated and equitable schools and institutional resources, it was clear that mainstream schooling institutions were not interested in a speedy pursuit of equity.[54] So, people committed to racial equity pursued Ethnic Studies in the 1960s, seeking some modicum of control over their education.

The fact that students of European descent have never been required to learn the histories that are taught in Ethnic Studies, while students of color are mandated to learn Anglo-European histories is nothing short of a hegemonic project of cultural supremacy.[55] The fact is that the curriculum and assessments used in the overwhelming majority of US public schools are not reflective of the student population, the broader society, or the world. Behind all the rhetoric of a global market economy and training students for the twenty-first-century workplace, there is very little happening in schools that suggests there is any intention to do this for the majority of students. Rhetorically speaking, this is "un-American" in every way, shape, and form. In reality, it is quintessentially "American" because there has never been a time in this country's history when it provided a high-quality education to all its citizens.[56]

FORWARD—HOW?

Just two days before my parents' sixty-second wedding anniversary, my father was killed in a car crash outside my parents' home.[57]

"What now?" I asked my mother, who was eighty-two years old at the time.

"I just have to remake myself, son. I will take each day as it comes and focus on what needs to be done. My glass is still half full," she replied.

She was simply repeating a lesson she taught me as a child when she ordered me to the kitchen table and placed a half-filled glass of water between us. Pointing at the glass, she asked, "Half full or half empty?" I refused the bait and stared blankly at the glass.

"Son," she continued, "how you choose to answer that question, is how you will live your life. Your glass will always be both half full and half empty. If you choose to see your life as half empty, focusing on the things you don't have, then you will never fill your cup. But, if you learn to see your life as half full, seeing all the things that you do have, then you will fill your cup, it will overflow, and you can share that with others."

The education of poor and working people in this country has often been treated as a glass half empty. For generations, we have rationalized why we haven't, why we won't, and why we can't serve "these" families. But, as my mother's lesson suggests, this is a choice that we make. It is not inevitable. We could, if we so desired, choose to see all children for their potential and invest in them accordingly. Were our nation to become serious about such an effort in education, we would, as my mother suggests, need to remake ourselves.

This remaking would begin with an honest accounting of the fact that the status quo approach to educating our children is failing miserably. We are not even close to meeting the needs of our student population. If not Ethnic Studies, then what? What is it that anti–Ethnic Studies factions suggest we do in schools? Their methods have failed for decades. All we hear is. "Keep it the way it is." Well, the way it is doesn't work for the vast majority of working-class and poor children, regardless of their ethnicity. Everyone knows this to be true.

Simply put, if you are not going to get down in the dirt with some new and creative ideas then step aside. The same people who toiled and labored to build this country will be the ones who save it from itself, and on that path they will humanize and value all people, regardless of their ethnic origins. That's Ethnic Studies. That's community responsiveness. That's relevance.

CHAPTER 6

RESPONSIBILITY

Equity for What?

What we say and what we do ultimately comes back to us so let
us own our responsibility, place it in our hands, and carry it with
dignity and strength.

—Gloria Anzaldúa, "Speaking in Tongues"

To build, maintain, and grow the relationships and the relevance
discussed in the previous two chapters, we need to have clar-
ity on our responsibility. In short, we will need to answer systemi-
cally and individually the question: Equity for what? Throughout
this book, I have made the argument that US public schools have
continually reified the status quo by investing in systems and practices that privilege the privileged. For a nation to do this in its public
schools is antithetical to a democracy; and in a country that has
so profoundly defiled, dehumanized, and discriminated against so
many, it has set us on a trajectory that is deeply problematic and
completely unsustainable. As renowned Irish poet William Butler
Yeats wrote in "The Second Coming," this center cannot hold.

The purpose of equity in the context in which I am discussing it here is the pursuit of justice, freedom, and truth telling for all of the children, families, and communities that have suffered under the yoke of this nation's irresponsibility. To arrive at this pursuit in the field of education, we will need to refocus our responsibility to ourselves, to our families, to our ancestors, to our community, to our nation, to our unborn children, and to our world. This refocus must put the emphasis of our work squarely onto serving those whom we have, from inception to present day, relegated to the shadowlands of our institutions of education. History will judge our schools like it judges any society. That judgment, while acknowledging fits and starts of progress and growth, will ultimately find us badly wanting based solely on how we have treated the most wounded ones in our society—because the true measure of a civilized society is how it takes care of those that are the most vulnerable. Schools are a social mirror, and that mirror reflects poorly on our society because we have been wholeheartedly dishonest about our intentions to leave no child behind. If we are to even begin to align our reality with our rhetoric, we will need to repurpose schools such that their primary responsibility is youth wellness. To accomplish this, we must align all five segments of our responsibility toward that end: purpose, people, program, practice, and the policy needed to support all of it.

PURPOSE

Were we to embrace the need for a major course correction in our society, we would rethink the purpose and responsibility of our schools generally, and specifically, the role of those institutions in the lives of the most vulnerable children. Reorienting our personal, institutional, and systemic responsibilities in this direction would demand that any time we get into a stuck place with a child, we pull out Maslow and sync it up with the First Nations model of wellness described in chapter 3. We would no longer locate the problem to be fixed in the child; for it is not our children who are broken but our institutions and the society that houses them. Instead, we would go again and again and again on our commitments to getting children what they need when they need it. I have seen too many educators who have a surface-level commitment to caring about the most wounded youth in our community. When those wounds present themselves in the inconvenient ways that they do, most educators step forward to offer support. But when the young person does not know how to receive that care in the way it is being presented, far too many educators take offense. They distance themselves from the child. They insist that they are there to help, and if the young person does not honor and respect that sacrifice, then there is nothing else to be done.

This, of course, is precisely the conclusion the young person is aiming to validate with their behavior, confirming by the very nature of the adult's rejection that there was no real intention to help in the first place—what Kohl referred to as "willed not-learning."[1] That is, young people (particularly our most wounded ones) can sense when what is being offered is what Brazilian educator Paulo Freire calls "false generosity" and they are not interested in that kind of support:

> Any attempt to "soften" the power of the oppressor in deference to the weakness of the oppressed almost always manifests itself in the form of false generosity; indeed, the attempt never goes beyond this. In order to have the continued opportunity to express their "generosity," the oppressors must perpetuate injustice as well. An unjust social order is the permanent fount of this "generosity," which is nourished by death, despair, and poverty. That is why the dispensers of false generosity become desperate at the slightest threat to its source.[2]

When young people sense that we are not responsive to delivering the kind of support that is concerned with the development of a loving, attached, and liberating relationship—what Freire calls "true generosity"—then they are right to reject what we are offering them. It is our duty to eliminate "the causes which nourish false charity. False charity constrains the fearful and subdued, the 'rejects of life,' to extend their trembling hands. True generosity lies in striving so that these hands—whether of individuals or entire peoples—need be extended less and less in supplication, so that more and more they become human hands which work and, working, transform the world."[3]

This would require a hard pivot from our education system, and that pivot can begin only with serious attention to designing schools and classrooms that are responsive to our society's historical and escalating levels of social inequality and child trauma. In my own such efforts as an educator, Antonia Darder's *Reinventing Paulo Freire: A Pedagogy of Love*, Jerry Tello's *Recovering Your Sacredness*, and Bruce Perry and Maia Szalavitz's *The Boy Who Was Raised as a Dog* have been beacons, illuminating insights and actionable solutions.[4] Darder's words, work, and wisdom have guided my practice as far back as I can remember. She has been a mentor, confidant, and Tía to so many of the critical educators I know. Her astute analysis of the conditions facing the nation's most dismissed and disconnected youth should be mandatory reading for every educator. As a student, mentee, and—dare I say—protégé of Paulo Freire, she has been the leading light in the transference of Freire's work into the US context.

Maestro Tello came into my life much later than Darder but has been just as influential. His work crafts a beautiful harmonizing of Indigenous medicine and Western clinical understandings to reveal a scholar-practitioner's vision for spaces that embrace and heal each one of us, returning us to the sacredness that our ancestors give all of us at our birth. His organization, The National Compadres Network, provides curriculum, support, and direct healing for countless educators and community members around the nation (myself included).

Perry is considered one of the leading clinical experts on child trauma, and his book helps us understand how exposure to toxic stress impacts the body, brain, and behavior of children and what we can do about it. Perry is the first medical expert I have heard refer to educators as first responders, holding down the frontline institutional response to child trauma. Our widespread failure to acknowledge this fact in the lives and preparation of teachers has resulted in a national crisis of teacher recruitment, job dissatisfaction, and early departure from the profession. It has also meant that our most wounded children, the children who most need our public schools, enter school and classroom environments that are ill-equipped to meet their most basic needs of mind, body, spirit, and emotion. The combined work of these three mentors, educators, and healers offers a powerful mixing of medicines that suggests our purposeful path forward must demand that wellness be the central and foundational purpose of our schools.

PEOPLE

Bettina Love, Athletic Association Endowed Professor at the University of Georgia, has called for abolitionist teaching in order to build classrooms that allow our children to do "more than survive."[5] She rightly argues that schools can and should be supporting the development of young people who are thriving and who are prepared to continue to thrive throughout their adult lives. In her concluding chapter of *We Want to Do More Than Survive*, Love insists that for "schools to be well, and therefore the children in them, schools must place more importance on students' mental, physical, and spiritual health than on any test. If students are not well, test scores do not matter."[6] It should not be lost on those who read Love's work that she is unapologetic and unrelenting in her insistence that this kind of wellness will not happen in schools without a profound commitment to uprooting the legacy and culture of white supremacy and anti-Blackness that permeates virtually every corner of our current public school project.

Christina Sharpe, in her book *In the Wake*, describes this omnipresence of white supremacy, particularly in the quotidian lives of Black people, as life in "the wake": . . . [T]he metaphor of the wake in the entirety of its meanings (the keeping watch with the dead, the path of a ship, a consequence of something, in the line of flight and/or sight, awakening, and consciousness."[7]

Sharpe's metaphor nearly perfectly describes the work that schools and educators must do if we are to meet the challenge of prioritizing youth wellness. To *keep watch* with the dead in education would require us to sit in the foundational cracks of our school system where broken spirits of children rest—those spirits sent to basements and bungalows, away from the deserving few, to live out their time in a system so flawed from its inception that it could not possibly see their humanity, let alone their potential. To keep watch in that space is to be a witness to the collateral damage of children thrown into the *wake/path* of schools as ships, full speed ahead with the project of shaming, sorting, and stationing young people ill-fitted for our society into their "proper place." Generations of children broken and laid bare are the *consequences* of our incessant quest to mask our false rigor, our punishment disguised as discipline, and our deep-seated desire to control their bodies, minds, and spirits. My own sons, and all those children who now find themselves taking their turn in the ship's wake, floating in this historically repetitive *line of flight and sight*, might well meet the same fate if they do not capitulate when their spirits tell them to question and resist. Every bit of the research indicates that these outcomes are guaranteed, no matter what kinds of reforms schools decide to make, unless there is an *awakening*—a radical shift in *consciousness* about the purpose of schools in our society.

The people who are needed to do this "wake work" are not people who have been introduced to this kind of suffering via books, mass media, or social media. Rather, they are the people who have experienced the particular needs that children present to us in schools. Over 80 percent of the national teaching force is white while less than 45 percent of the public school student population is white, and all indicators suggest that the number of white students will continue to decline precipitously.[8] This is not to say that white teachers cannot effectively teach students of color. I would not say this any more than I would argue that teachers of color would be ineffective with white children. Rather, the point here is that these demographics of the US teaching force are both troubling and out of step with the demographic reality of the nation if we recognize the extensive research that concludes that the ethnicity of the teacher has measurable impact on engagement and achievement for students of color.[9] This same argument can, and should, be made for administrators and educational leaders writ large.

For this nation to live up to its lofty ideals, it would demand of us the courage to confront what Baldwin calls the "principal facts" of our shortcomings and a commitment to the creativity to correct them.[10] Were we to engage such an endeavor, schools would need to play a significantly different role in our society, shifting from reinforcing the status quo to redefining it. Any such discussion of creating schools that prepare young people to take on the seemingly intractable forms of inequity facing our society will require us to seriously rethink our ideals for the people working inside of them. To recruit, support, develop, and sustain a new class of educator, the national commitment to the teaching profession must radically shift and be seamlessly aligned with the repurposing of schools.

This new direction for educators must pay closer attention to the research on the social indicators of health if we are going to prepare educators to meet the challenges of working in the wake. To this end, we must examine some of the most cutting-edge, and also some of the most established, research in fields such as public health, community psychology, social epidemiology, and medical sociology to improve adult learning for educators so that they might be better equipped to do wake work. This approach constitutes a re-thinking of our approach toward one that aims to develop educators better equipped to respond to the "socially toxic environments" that emerge from white supremacy, class supremacy, hetero-supremacy, male supremacy, and all other forms of oppression.[11] Given the abysmal performance record of schools serving our nation's most impoverished youth, it seems high time that those of us working to prepare teachers and leaders for those schools heed Baldwin's advice and take a long look at ourselves. What we are doing is not working, and if we are honest, we will admit that it has not been working for some time—it could even be reasonably argued that it has never worked *or* that it is all working perfectly to plan.[12]

Recent research breakthroughs in the aforementioned fields have turned their attention to identifying and understanding the social indicators of health and well-being; for education, this is the idea that "place"—the conditions in which our students live—must be understood for teachers to be effective.[13] This research reveals clearly identifiable social toxins that young people face in the broader society and these are the "principal facts" that we must prepare educators to confront. Drawing from these analyses, the next section lays out the program and pedagogical framework educators can use to be more community responsive, treating the classroom as a micro-ecosystem committed to "radical healing" and "critical hope."[14]

PROGRAM

I have said on any number of occasions that programs don't work. People work. This was never meant to imply that programs do not matter. Of course they matter. But what I have watched time and again is efforts to McDonaldize the education of children using the language of "effective programs." Of course, this happens most commonly with the children whom our school systems continually fail in an effort to avoid any real and critical systemic self-reflection. Instead, shortcuts are deployed, and when they inevitably fail (because there are no shortcuts to doing right by vulnerable children), hands are wrung and promises proffered that this same program worked in some other place with a "similar group of students." This essentializing of the needs and cultures of children of color is endemic to a white supremacist system of schooling that never intended to respond to the lives, needs, cultures, and languages of the communities it was designed to Americanize via repression, indoctrination, and domestication.[15]

Any given school can, and should, be seeking out evidence of effective programs in its surrounding communities and also in the national landscape. This has become increasingly possible for school leaders who are intentional about learning and designing programs that are community responsive. The number of organizations available to educators who are looking to identify, link, and build with other similarly committed educators has grown significantly in the last decade: H20 Productions, Pin@y Educational Partnership (PEP), Roses in Concrete Community School, National Compadres Network, People's Education Movement, Black Teacher Project, Abolitionist Teaching Network (ATN), New York Collective of Radical Educators (NYCORE), and Teachers for Social Justice (T4SJ) to name a few. These connections do not guarantee anything, except the opportunity to learn. There is no perfect playbook. There is no flawless formula. By accessing other similarly committed people and programs, what can be unveiled is a set of principles and values that guide the design, implementation, integrity, and sustainability of success. The success of those values and practices rests on the people upholding and implementing them.

This is where the fault line sits. The search for a quick programmatic fix to correct centuries of disinvestment designed to undermine the well-being of a community will always crack under the pressures brought about by that very design. If schools want to learn from success, the focus of their inquiry needs to be threefold: (1) What is the foundational intent and purpose of the work that worked? (2) What principles and practices undergirded the pursuit of that intent and purpose? and (3) Who were the people who were most successful in implementing those principles and practices, and why were those people effective?

The idea that we can lift out successful practice from a predominantly Latinx community and transport it to another predominantly Latinx community is not only ignorant, it is racist. It presumes any number of things that sit at the heart of white supremacist thinking, including but not limited to, the belief that all [insert POC group] people are the same. We see this in large-scale, white-led efforts that pimp the suffering of children of color in the languishing public school systems across the nation (see KIPP, Aspire, and Teach for America as a few larger-scale examples). These organizations have spent decades sucking down trillions of dollars in community resources while offering fool's gold to vulnerable communities under the assumption that they can do the colonial model of schooling better than the local district schools. Virtually nothing about any of these organizations or their approach to education for non-dominant groups is aligned with wake work. There is no organizational intention or collective purpose to dismantle the colonial legacy of white supremacy in their projects and, as a result, their impact remains nominal at best, despite their self-aggrandizing claims about transforming the lives of our children en masse.

PRACTICE

In order to design the community-responsive practices that children need, educators must be prepared to answer three core questions: (1) What are the material conditions that affect the youth being served before they even step foot in our hallways and classrooms? (2) What does it mean to develop educational environments that are caring, relevant, and responsive to these conditions and the historical realities that created them? (3) What supports are necessary in teacher recruitment, training, and support to develop educators and school leaders that create this type of school and classroom practice? Answers to these questions pose a challenge that must be met with vigor in every school, and the approach to such efforts must be specific to the context where that work is taking place. Much of the discussion offered in this book is aimed at developing program and practice that prioritizes the most wounded and vulnerable children. Most, if not all, of these approaches are applicable for educators working in contexts of relative privilege, although I would argue they must be adjusted for that context by similarly committed experts in those communities.

Efforts to answer these questions with our community, and to support other communities to do the same, are the essence of this book. Much of this responsibility that I feel as an educator requires that I return to ancestral medicines for guidance—a deep well of wisdom available to all of us should we choose to go looking there. I do not think I am going to write anything here about shifting school and classroom practices that is not already coursing through your blood and deeply embedded in your DNA and your consciousness. So, my hope is that this call to our individual and collective responsibility to shift our practice is as affirming as it is instructive for us to create spaces that are truly community responsive for the children and families that need us the most such that meeting this responsibility taps into the best of our sensibilities.

There is a way in which Western medicine, and dominant institutions generally, have suddenly been forced to recognize the wellness-wisdom of people of color. And so, suddenly many people (and the institutions they govern) who have ignored, and even outright rejected, that wisdom are now proclaiming they have discovered it as a provable truth. This, of course, is an essential part of the colonial model—to denigrate and discard the ancestral-cultural practices of those being otherized to justify their dehumanization and then resurfacing those same practices as discoveries made by settler colonialists. Nevertheless, we find ourselves in a moment where at least some of the nation is beginning to look our way for some of the answers they have been unable to find using the colonial model. After all, what better place to look for the medicine to survive a pandemic than from the communities that you have kept trapped in pandemic for centuries? Indigenous and Black folks specifically, and other folks of color generally, have been forced to survive the global pandemics of colonialism and white supremacy for hundreds of years. So, in a kind of weird, sick, colonial, white-supremacist, male-supremacist, hetero-supremacist, and class-supremacist twist of fate, we have landed on a profound moment of opportunity to transform. This may very well be the moment where we stop *asking* for our children to be well and we start *telling* how that birthright will be restored. And the more we know, the more ammunition that we have to support the practices that have allowed our people, our families, our young people, and our land to endure these pandemics.

In this moment, we can more effectively push those into play in the corridors of power and reclaim ways that are self-determining and autonomous to build and sustain the wellness of all of our children.

The time is long overdue to completely repurpose schools by making youth wellness the foundational practice of schools in this nation—youth wellness not as a program, not as an add-on, not as a class, but as *the* sole purpose of why we send our babies into these institutions for seven hours a day for thirteen consecutive years. It is inexcusable that any child, but particularly the most vulnerable and the most wounded children, would leave school less well than when they walked through the doors. The time for asking schools to see us, hear us, and serve us has long since passed. We are not asking. We are telling. We are telling that this is the purpose of the institutions to which we are sending our children. And if it is not, then we are not going to send our children there anymore. This is our human right. There could be no greater indignity than for Native people (whose land those schools sit on) and Black people (who built so much of this nation and its economy without compensation under the yoke of white slave masters) to be forced to send their children to institutions that contribute to their collective suffering. But in order to pull this off in practice, the defining of wellness cannot be left to the dominant culture that has, heretofore, acted as gatekeepers to definitions and guardians of the dictionaries that sanction and sustain them. We have to be community self-determining and define for these institutions what we mean when we say wellness for our children.

In our community, a group of us have undertaken just such an effort to define and measure the wellness of our children. After nearly a year of work across cultural and ethnic communities of youth, families, elders, teachers, indigenous healers, clinicians, and researchers, we landed on this definition of wellness as the starting part for our work to center youth wellness in schools:

Wellness is the harmonizing of mind, body, emotion and spirit. It is cultivated and sustained through healthy relationships that are responsive to the lived experiences and the historical and material conditions that shape them. Community responsive wellness strengthens the sacred link between self-actualization and community actualization in three domains: 1. Innerself: a strong sense of culture, identity, and agency; 2. Interpersonal: a rootedness and commitment to showing empathy toward family, community, and peers; and 3. Interconnectedness: positive interrelatedness to ancestors, place, land, and the natural world. This grows ecosystems where people and communities experience place, power, purpose, awareness, resilience, empathy, hope, love, and joy.[16]

There are four elements of wellness in this definition: mind, body, emotion, and spirit. It is important to acknowledge that for the purposes of this discussion of wellness, these different elements are called out, but in practice they should be treated as highly intersectional and interdependent. In other words, relationships, actions and energies that are medicine for the mind might very well be medicine for the body, emotion, and spirit. This cuts both ways, as attacks on the mind will run throughout all elements of a person's wellness and, by extension, a community's wellness. It is all connected, and we are all connected. This does not preclude us from discussing layers and elements of wellness, but any sort of discussion we have about making the wellness of our children the priority of our practice must understand that it is all interconnected.

The three domains (innerself, interpersonal, interconnectedness) are also very much interrelated. But for the purposes of designing practices that create a climate and culture that develops each domain among youth, they can be thought of as more distinct. This work toward wellness really begins with the innerself, and the work of the innerself begins with young people and families being able to tell their own stories—to see their own sacredness.[17] This self-love is a natural outgrowth of the acknowledgment of all the gifts that have been afforded us at birth because of our ancestors. The depth of this self-love brings with it an understanding about our own value and, by default, expands our capacity to develop meaningful and attached interpersonal relationships with other people.

The second domain is focused on these interpersonal connections with other people. The ability to connect more deeply within our immediate circles expands our capacity to do so beyond those circles. When we connect deeply with others, we are mixing our medicines. This becomes much more possible and potent when a person knows that they have medicine, what that medicine is, and where it comes from. An approach to practice where the innerself is bridged to the interpersonal is foundational for all children, but especially for those children who experience a broader society that explicitly and implicitly undermines the message of their sacredness. This is why Ethnic Studies is so important, and this is why Ethnic Studies is so intently focused on the narratives and histories of people of color. When the light of the innerself is turned on, interpersonal relationships are healthier and more likely to be centered in love, care, respect, and connection. Thus, practices that lead youth to know their histories, cultures, and traditions give them the gift of being in relationship with their own medicine. When these practices are extended to bring young people into relationship with others, it permits a mixing of medicines such that all of those involved have their respective medicines made even more powerful. Some of the things being taught in school are also forms of medicine in that they are cultural narratives and markers. But because so many children are asked to check their culture (their medicine) at the door, the opportunity to mix medicines in school is lost. What happens instead is that youth develop a relationship with school where the "medicine" is shoved down their throats rather than shared with them and they are then told that it is good for their future. This approach does not make anybody feel well.

The third domain is interconnectedness, which describes the ways that we connect to the cosmos, Mother Earth, and our ancestors. This domain is attentive to the kinds of relationships we have with trees, animals, insects, and the entire natural environment and it influences the interplay between our internal and interpersonal wellness. Ultimately, this kind of practice is aimed at growing ecosystems where people and communities experience place, power, purpose, awareness, resilience, empathy, hope, love, and joy. Frankly, that is all I want schools talking about for the foreseeable future. Everything else that we might think we want to teach—the mechanical skills of reading, writing, and arithmetic—can be taught with these things as the central purpose. Instead, we have taught generations of children these mechanical skills without the explicit intention of using them to deepen our wellness. This is the great tragedy of our society, and it is the foundation of our toxic culture.

Several months ago, I was meeting with a room full of school principals and superintendents, and we were having this discussion about the purpose of schools. To illustrate this point about our responsibility to shift the purpose, people, program, practice, and policy, I told them that I was going to take them through an exercise used in survey research known as "forced choice." Forced choice is a type of survey question that requires the respondent to select only one from among a group of choices where there are multiple desirable options. The idea is that it "forces" the respondent to identify their true priorities. This was to be a one-question survey of these leaders, and I asked them to answer the question with their own children in mind, rather than the children served by their institution(s), or as Lisa Delpit so aptly put it, "other people's children."[18] The question for them to answer was:

Choose between the following two options: Option A: Your children score in the ninetieth percentile on nationally accepted measurements of reading, writing, and arithmetic, but they score in the bottom quartile of measurements of wellness. Option B: Your children score in the ninetieth percentile on wellness measures, but in the bottom quartile of nationally accepted measurements of reading, writing, and arithmetic.

I asked the room to privately write down their selection in their notebooks: A or B. Then, I asked that everyone who chose option A to raise their hand. No one did. When I asked "Who chose option B?", everyone raised their hand.

I told them I would choose the same. That decision makes total sense to me. If my two sons are not well, I really do not care if they are reading, writing, and doing math on grade level. If they are well and they are behind on some measure of their ability to do any of those things, then I know that it is just a matter of time before we find the best way to catch them up if that is truly what they want for their lives. I also know that if they learn to live in wellness, it does not really matter whether they latch onto a particular rote academic skill because they will find the only thing I really want for them, which is for them to be happy, healthy, and pursuing their sacred purpose.

Finally, I asked the principals to share how they measure these things that they care about so much for their children in the institutions where they are the leaders. No one raised their hand. We measure what matters, I told them. Angela Duckworth told me once, "We measure what we treasure." Actually, we do neither; or maybe we do both under a double standard. Regardless of how we analyze this situation, the truth is that because we do not measure the things that matter most for youth wellness, we end up with institutional practices that pay little more than lip service to the wellness of our children. When we do start to turn our gaze in that direction, it is frequently reactionary (as in the case of school shootings) or superficial (as in the case of social-emotional programs whose primary intent is to force children to regulate/control/repress the emotions that emerge out of their suffering).[19] Both of these are efforts on the part of schools to sanitize the classroom and school environment, and at the end of the day, the focus remains on the same measurements we have always tracked.

None of this is to say that reading, writing, and arithmetic do not matter. What a hypocrite I would be, sitting here writing a book with "PhD" after my name, to say that those things do not matter. But any psychometrician would tell us that the things that we continue to emphasize in our measurement and data conversations (formative and summative assessment scores, attendance, discipline, GPA) are overwhelmingly lagging indicators of student development. The leading indicators of youth development are the indicators of wellness, and we simply do not measure these things with any real rigor or respect for their significance to the long-term health of the child and our society. The result is that no matter what we might tell school leaders, teachers, children, and families about school being a safe and caring place that is committed to the well-being of our children, it is not. We can put slogans up on every wall, but this does not change the fact that we are telling people what matters by what we measure (and by what we do not measure). Nowhere is this clearer than in how we respond to the children who are the most vulnerable and the most wounded; the children whom we send to the schools with the fewest resources, the least-supported teachers, the most antiquated pedagogical practices, and the most dilapidated and dysfunctional environments. There is no reason for them to believe that we care about their well-being because we prove, time and again, what it is that we actually care about by the things we invest in and measure in our practice.

POLICY

We cannot policy our way out of this mess that we are in. As with program, this does not mean that policy does not matter. I was in the classroom before No Child Left Behind (NCLB), during NCLB, and after NCLB. I can say unequivocally that that policy impacted my practice. Policy is not benign, but policy will not save us. It can certainly make it much easier for us to meet the responsibilities to children discussed in this chapter, or it can make it much more challenging. The primary problem with educational policy is the lack of proximity that policy makers have to the pains of practice. Until the most vulnerable communities are the ones that are setting the policy agenda for schools, there is virtually no possibility that policy will support the changes in practice that are necessary for schools to be truly community responsive. In short, communities must set the policy agenda instead of policy setting the agenda for communities. There is no other way.

CLOSING THE KNOWING-DOING GAP: WHAT DOES RESPONSIBILITY LOOK LIKE IN PRACTICE?

In this section of closing the knowing-doing gap, I am sharing an interview that I did with Tiffani Marie. I have known Tiffani since 2005 when she was one of my first students at San Francisco State University. I can think of very few people who have so profoundly and consistently influenced my thinking, my practice, and the way I live my life. She is the kind of human being I want my sons to be around as often as possible—I can pay no higher compliment. She is a brilliant artist, orator, creative, researcher, teacher, colleague, and friend. I chose to interview her for the responsibility section of this book because for the entirety of our relationship, she has continued to ask the questions that get at the very purpose of our existence as teachers.

The second example for this section is a reflection on an experience from my own classroom practice that shaped, and continues to reshape, my understanding about my responsibility as an educator. This moment came much later in my teaching career, so it also serves as an ever-present reminder for me that, like life, teaching is a journey that is never finished. Teaching is an art form that will humble you, especially if you become complacent in your craft. To be a teacher is one of the highest honors that can be bestowed on the human species and it therefore demands great responsibility from us. This is so because we are all teachers of children. They are watching us—both word and deed—and they are learning. Some of us are called to embrace this path as our sacred purpose. We hone this time-honored craft, as did those who came before us on this path. Those who knowingly make this choice have an even greater responsibility to look for, listen to, and embrace the lessons that children offer us. The story that I share at the end of this chapter is one of the most important lessons about my responsibility as a teacher that a young person has ever shared with me.

H2O Productions and Apocalyptic Ed

Tiffani Marie is the daughter of Sheryll Marie, granddaughter of Dorothy Wilson and Annette Williams, and great-granddaughter of Artelia Green and Olivia Williams.[20] She comes from a long line of Arkansas educators. At her best, Tiffani is immersed within beloved community, producing music and sewing. Her current research examines the cumulative biopsychosocial impacts of stress on Black bodies and the types of critical pedagogical practices that attenuate the harmful impacts of toxic stress in Black youth. Her life's work is committed to curating spaces of healing and sustained health for

Black people. What follows is an edited transcript of an interview that I conducted with her for this section of this book.

JDA: *Can you share a bit about your ancestral and personal history and how that brought you into working with young people?*

TIFFANI MARIE: What I've been talking to a lot of folks about recently is this title that people have been saying and using to describe me: Dr. Tiffani Marie Johnson. I think when people truly are critical about it and look at me and think about that title, then they'll truly understand a lot of the violence that contributed to me entering teaching, but also just being here on these lands. That's been really fundamental for me to think about as it relates to getting here. So much in my life, like my name—which, if I were actually born on the lands that are indigenous to my people, would probably be something like Yaa Marie. And so the idea of Dr. Tiffani Marie Johnson is this interesting sandwiching of the violences that have happened, and then the center is all questionable. But what is very real and concrete is my time in the academy and then this branding of whoever this Johnson person is. And that to me is really important and it's really connected to my ancestral roots in that I more than likely (and I have to say "more than likely") come from the Akan people and I have roots with Yoruba folks in what we know as Nigeria.

So, I know that my folks, both sides of my family, end up in Arkansas some time after they were forcefully brought here. I come from a lot of cultivators of land and canners—people who canned food and grew food. I also come from a lot of teachers, particularly classroom teachers. So, this interesting thing happened with a lot of my cousins who grew up in Arkansas. They had all this knowledge (from the ancestors) but the thrust and the force for them to be in schools influenced them to leave home, so none of the generation before me, or my generation, still live there on those lands. They're all in major cities. So, a lot of what we knew and where we came from has been lost. And so much of what we have been taught over the years about what it means to bring pride to our family has been associated with success in schools. That has been the language on both sides of my family. So, it was natural for me to desire that and pursue it vigorously, and that is what I've been doing.

When I left undergrad, I really actually didn't have any desire to teach. I had the desire to make a lot of money. I tell people I wanted to be just like Oprah. I wanted to be this expert on Black people and what they need to do for themselves in whatever way that I needed to in order to live the way that I see her live.

Then I took your class, which was life-altering. I wept in that first class because it was in that class where I realized how deep the self-hate was. In one class. I was like, well, that's a powerful skill to have. To help people access that type of consciousness. It was that class that activated for me a critical memory of who and where I come from. Ever since then I've been desiring—and of course there has been a lot of failure in that process—but I've been trying to help people to remember more and more about themselves and the way that I received that, particularly from your graduate-level class.

JDA: *I don't think you've ever told me that story. At least not in that way. Thank you for sharing that with me. Can you share a bit about the work that you are currently engaged in, and your hopes for how it might impact non-dominant communities generally and young people specifically?*

TIFFANI MARIE: The current work, really just from the past eighteen months, is seeming like a huge pivot. But it's not. It's a returning. But it's seeming like a huge pivot from what I've been doing for thirteen years. The current work is really connected to how I ended that last question. It's really just about remembering. Not from this generic space. Toni Morrison talks about it in "The Site of Memory." She talks about how in Mississippi there were establishments built alongside the river, and people every year prepare themselves for this thing called "flooding." And it's seen as this disastrous act. I love how she talks about the flooding as the word that some of us use, but others use the word "remember." Our memory. It's just the water's attempt to return to what we know.

I like to think of what we're doing right now in a very similar vein in that we use the term "Apocalyptic Ed," and it seems really disastrous what we're doing. It seems like we're pulling the rug from certain people, but I really see that as "the flooding," the word that people use to describe what we are doing, but in actuality it is just an attempt to return to what we know and who we were. So that centers language revitalization for ourselves as educators, but for our young people as well. It centers a return to the natural world. We used to do field trips, but now it is more of a foundational component where it's not extra to us. The system even has this language where they would call that *extra* curricular. To us, it *is* curriculum, with its own pedagogical practice for our young people to return to the natural world. There's so much emphasis in what we're trying to do through our relationships, particularly with the trees. It's such an interdisciplinary process that seems so fulfilling now.

In the past, I've left with a certain fatigue that reflected my spirit's uncertainty. Now I leave with a certain satisfaction that I have never felt in this practice. It is really just about memory. So much of what we're doing and what I'm finding in our research is that this is really antithetical to schooling. So, in one of our first weeks, our Latinx kids were learning Nahuatl from these Nahuatl teachers in Mexico, and they were getting these classes via Zoom. This is before quarantine. So, our kids are gathered, they're super pumped, they're huddled around this computer . . . and these are juniors, and they're singing their songs. And it's very embodied, so they're standing up and sitting down when that's what the instructor suggests they should do in Nahuatl. And the AP Spanish teacher busts in the room and she just starts screaming at the kids. We had already sent an email and asked, letting her know that once a month this was going to conflict with her class. Here's the schedule, let us know if there are any issues with it. She says nothing to us, comes right when the Nahuatl class in session, busts open, and my co-teacher had to actually stand between her and the kids because she was walking toward the kids. And this is someone they really respect. This is a teacher that they honor. And it was just—they were taken aback by the irony of the situation. They're sitting there learning their indigenous language, and this woman is saying, "You are missing the Advanced Placement course of your colonizer's language." And we just had to sit in that. This is a person who, on the side, would agree with us that our kids need to know this [Nahuatl]. And in practice, she was like, "This got to end right now." If we would have allowed her, she would have pulled on their clothes and made them come into her classroom. I'm confident. So much of what we've been doing has made teachers mad or upset. But, when you really center these acts of memory, which we also call acts of wellness and health, the structure as it exists is compromised greatly.

JDA: *Can you describe the high school program that you've been running for the last several years?*

TIFFANI MARIE: We call it H2O Productions, and this is its fourth or fifth iteration. But it got that name when I started a group called "The Square Kids." It started when we were at this assembly and this little Black girl—dark, dark Black girl—who had gotten an award for the Principal's Honor Roll or something, and she was so embarrassed to walk to the front of the school to be celebrated. It bothered me so much. So, I went home and I decided to start this rap group called "the Square Kids" that celebrated achievement or whatever generic thing we thought was cool at the time. So, they had songs and they had videos, and it blew up. Their YouTube videos had thousands of hits. Some kids actually would tell their parents they wanted to come to our school because of Square Kids. One of the original Square Kids was in the car and he was freestyling and "H2O, yeah that's water" . . . he just kept saying that. So we took that name for our work. And it's so deep to think about what I said earlier about what Toni Morrison said about water, because back then we really thought of our young people as clay because they are so impressionable. And what I started to notice about Play-Doh and clay when we would play with it was that, depending on the environment it was in, it could dry out. And when it dries out, it's really fragile and it just breaks. And the component that would always revitalize your clay was water. So, whatever has happened to you, we acknowledged that things have happened to us, that have broken us, and we wanted our organization to be that agent that actually loosens you back up into a position to be able to get into stretch zones to be able to exist, to live, and not just live but to live abundantly.

So, H2O started when I was volunteering, and I took on a cohort. And that was right when I learned about your cohort model. We emulated that, to be very transparent. Our work was informed by some of the models that I had studied with you, but also really just my love of critical pedagogy and art. So, we centered Youth Participatory Action Research. We wanted to ensure that our young people traveled, that they investigated their lived experiences. But some of the teaching in our program also centered their public speaking. In the first iteration, we very much believed that if young people had critical analysis of the environments that they lived in, that would inform their agency and the decisions that they made. If they had caring adults around them, they would be held in that process. And we could serve as a greater buffer against those other forces that we had no control over. And at the end of that, we very much centered college matriculation as a sign of success from their time with us.

After our second iteration of H2O, we had it. We had 100 percent college matriculation. We surveyed all the kids in our senior class, and our kids had the highest scores on the Children's Hope

Scale. They had the highest attendance, and we felt really successful in those models until the following year, when almost 45 percent of our kids were no longer in college after one year. The ones who did stay were suffering; they didn't feel good. And so much of our work became responding to their needs on these campuses that were much deeper than what we could provide. Since then, many of them have graduated from college and we noticed the void in what our young people were needing, even with those college degrees. And so, though this last iteration has really centered the well-being of young people and not using trauma-informed pedagogy or critical pedagogy as this carrot to get them to do school better, but really just centering . . . how do you ensure . . . I think Linda (Tuhiwai) Smith said it years ago: "First, how do you prevent death in your work? And then, how do you create structures, frameworks, and paradigms for young people in which they actually are healthier?"

So, this latest iteration of our work, which I am saying is the fifth, began to engage these Western measurements of wellness as a way to affirm our hunches, which were coming from our ancestral traditions. So that's really just been looking at telomeres, oxytocin, and engaging neuroscience to look at activity in the parietal lobe to really just affirm spiritually what we already know we should be doing.

JDA: *So, how would you describe the pedagogical framework that guides your teaching? Specifically, I'm asking about the "how." You talked about critical pedagogy, you talked about YPAR, travel . . . How did you do it? What did you do? And why were you choosing those things as your guides?*

TIFFANI MARIE: Well, the what, why, and how have changed. What we were doing initially was creating a structure for students to do well academically, as measured by GPA. So, we had interesting and engaging classes. And why I say "critical pedagogy" in particular is because the "critical" in it is an acknowledgment of a history of violence that I think is very different from a lot of people's approaches. Our work was really intentional around both acknowledging the history of violence that led to us speaking English to each other so well and inside of a building whose architecture literally blocks us from the natural world. So, we had to engage that, and that's what made a lot of it critical. Young people developed an analysis of their own oppression and of the world that they live in. It was a very Freirian praxis, developing these types of plans for transformative action and how they would work to take back their own lives and their own well-being, and also hoping that they accepted a social responsibility to do that within and for their communities as well. So, that would come from the readings. It would come from the content they experienced in our classroom. There was this desire to engage them with telling the truth, providing a number of counternarratives, content, and stories that our young people had rarely, if ever, experienced in their schooling. Outside of that, there was the tutorial structure where we wanted to create space where they were held in how and when they were able to do the work, and in what capacity, through caring community. And then when you talk about the travel—initially, it was still very much a way for them to see what else exists in the world as a way to inspire them to come back and desire upward mobility. It was like, "See, if you make more money, then you can go see all these things. Isn't this great?" And the entire model was still very capitalist. We were still in Airbnbs and still, ironically, supporting the very structures and systems that we were critiquing in our class. We were centering school requirements and not young people's health. And we were hoping that, by centering those, it would lead to their success within schools. And I think it's sometimes taught in public health that that centering actually negatively impacts social determinants of health. All of this presumed that, just by matriculating in here, you would have access to a greater life. As we continued, we realized that that's just not true for people who look like me. This came from some of my fatigue, but also from some of the people who I was working with.

And then, thinking about many of the Black women who I really value, and they died younger than fifty. They were college graduates. They were published authors. Then I started realizing that many of these women that were in education were breast cancer survivors. And so there was a gaping wound, or hole, in this argument around more school equals better health. All of that hit us really hard after that second or third iteration of H2O. We were just, like, this is not playing out how we envisioned it. So, when we did this latest iteration, we actually centered the health of young people. What that meant for us was to be open to the idea that there was a lot that we needed to learn, even though that was year eleven for me. I had to be open to being a baby again; to learning and depending on folks. And also, to being really open to what our young people had to say and were experiencing. So, very early on the commitments and the partnerships that we made were with health practitioners, elders, and Indigenous healers to inform how we did the work. So, their freshman year, yes, we traveled. But we traveled to Aotearoa, New Zealand, to be able to learn from folks. We brought the young people with us and it wasn't like we had a plan. The kids had presentations to share, but that's not actually what happened when we went there.

I would say that trip kind of set the stage for a lot more of the disruption that would happen within our vision and our pedagogical practices. When we were there, so much of what our kids engaged in was not part of a plan. For example, we had these plans to have our young people finish this assignment for work they were doing back home and for something we had planned for the next day. And all of that was shut down because that evening was about the release—because earlier that day, we did Romiromi, the Maori deep tissue massage that releases trauma. After our kids and our teachers were on those tables and experiencing these deep tissue responses, that changed . . . not just the landscape of the evening, but what we knew we had to do when we got back.

When we did get back, it was a continuation of how do we center these practices and how do we listen to what comes out of these practices to inform content and curriculum? So much of that has informed our trips—and we don't even call them trips . . . they inform our classroom practice, except our classrooms are not within the confines of the school. Now, our classrooms are when we go to the Yuba River, when we go bike riding, and it became desired. Not just by us, but by our young people. The taste of it, and how normative it was, meant they literally could no longer do school in the same way. Their scholarship was profoundly impacted by them feeling and being better.

For the "why" . . . we already had these hunches. We had a lot of fights and arguments with certain kids around getting them to sit down, getting them to do school in this way, and a lot of harm was caused. A lot! Luckily, I'm still in relationship with those kids to hear about it and to be healthy enough as an adult to be humble enough to listen to that critique. We had these hunches, but as we continued, we literally began to see what was happening to their bodies. And that was the game changer. We had already taken saliva samples from kids, but we didn't know what impact we were having just based on what we were experiencing. But, when we got those results to see what was happening to the bodies of fourteen-year-olds, or what had happened to the bodies of fourteen-year-olds and to see that they had stress comparable to women who were triple their age . . . that was a game changer. We ended up breaking [research] protocol later, but I wanted to break protocol right then because I was like, "We need to know who these kids are. We need to jump and hold these kids right now." And I remember my co-teacher said, "What would it be like if we imagine that this was every kid? That these were the results of every kid?" So, we didn't break protocol at that time. We just assumed it was everyone. We didn't know who it was, so everybody was going to get this critical, urgent intervention. We stopped caring about people's opinions. We had spent a lot of time trying to convince people, their teachers, to be okay with what we were choosing to do. When we saw those results and we knew that our children were dying . . . they were literally dying . . . so much shifted. The irony, I think, and one of the greatest lessons, is that we thought we would be losing so much learning time because we needed to respond with this like triage. And that's wrong. That's wrong. That response to their bodies actually rendered and cultivated an open space for the greatest learning and teachings that I've ever been involved in.

JDA: *Can you talk about the roles that relationships and relevance played in your pedagogical approach?*

TIFFANI MARIE: We now call our pedagogical approach "Apocalyptic Ed." That's the language we are using right now. It starts from the premise . . . it centers this story in *Krik? Krak!* One of my favorite stories, "Children of the Sea," where these Haitians are migrating to the States and the boat that they're in has a hole in it. The boat is sinking. And there's this character, Célianne, who, as a teenager, is giving birth to this baby. So much of the short story is around her caretaking of the baby and this secret that everybody on the boat is just sitting in. The secret was that she had been caring for—or tending to, really—all this time, a dead baby.

The baby was stillborn, and she just was not ready to acknowledge it or deal with the death that was in front of her. But the ship is sinking and folks on the ship are throwing all of the nonessentials overboard and they're looking at her like "Yo, we're sorry, but it's time to go." And I forgot about that. I read that as a teenager, and it came back to me about how similar our practices are as educators as it relates to our relationship to the actual school. What we say in our work is that we do think kids are dying on our watch. But the dead baby that we are trying to make connections on is school. And so much tending has gone to the actual building and the practices within it, to uphold that. We start from the premise that those are dead. And we start there because of our history as Black people in these spaces. Our histories are very telling. In our histories, plantations and ships were our first schools, and really the wood from those sites just extended into the actual institution that our kids are in today. We went through that critical memory and we situated our pedagogy there, and that informs our decisions.

So, when we start from the premise that schools are actually dead, that they're the architecture that has and will continue to prevent us from real classrooms, it informs what we teach the young people and what we even deem as relevant. If we start with the ship, or even the slave plantation as a school, then we're not going to be focused on kids learning how to be more successful in the house. That's just not our goal. And that may be a position that kids occupy because some of their ancestors did strategically. But our focus is not for you to be more successful there.

What has been fundamental for me was learning about maroon communities that existed outside of the plantation that were able to maintain their indigenous practices. These are folks who either got off boats and were out immediately, or actually touched plantations and were like, "We have to go." Who set up shop alongside it and maintained these really sustainable lives. And so *that* is what we deem is relevant in our relevancy. What are the tools and practices that we can pass on to our young people so that they can exist outside? I think sometimes we don't even give that as an option to young people. It's as if we frame our entire approach like "It's gonna be painful, getting into the house is going to be painful, so I'm gonna give you these tools." For us, we're just trying to imagine, and to actualize, what it is that we need to exist around right now. So that center, of course, informs the type of relationship that we have with our young people. So in the past, I would be this "warm demander." That is the term that people use. Or we can say a benevolent dictator, or a kind slave master. It's a matter of the language that people want to use, but that used to be our relationship with young people, and they felt better about it because it was people that looked like them. Because I wore gold fronts, because I have J's too . . . I actually think that's more violent and more confusing to children.

So much of our relationships have shifted because the relevance has shifted in that what we find relevant, and the most relevant. This is the game changer for me. Like can you, which I can't, tell time by looking at the sun? Can you grow your own food? Do you know the languages necessary for you to meditate in to access the ancestral realm? Do you have the tools and resources necessary to heal yourself? Where does your medicine come from? So, if you have a headache, do you take ibuprofen versus make your own tinctures? Not just that, but do you even see value in making your own tinctures? So, all of these things inform the relationships that we have with young people. So, what I have truly realized is that so much of our work is human centered. Human centric. What this shift in relevancy has revealed for me is the need for relationship; not just with other human beings but relationship to the natural world.

This sister wrote this poem that I read the other day, that two years ago I would have said was garbage. But one of the lines was, "What was the last thing you learned from the moon?" Those types of questions inform the types of relationships that we have with young people. I think most teenagers know that adults lie to them. Some of them have forgiven me in the past. They know how I was pushing higher ed was some nonsense. They know it. But they trusted me in certain ways and forgave me when I was being violent. But this work and this reconnection to the Earth, the reconnection to the natural world, the starting place that schools are dead . . . I think kids already know that. So, they believe us, they trust us, and they engage with us in fundamentally different ways because they're like, "Finally. Finally, someone has the starting place that we have been right in our resistance for all these years. And now what?" There's a lot to say about that, but that's what came to me when you asked that question.

JDA: *Can you think of an example of a young person, or group of young people, that embody what you just described?*

TIFFANI MARIE: One example is when we went to Kia Aroha.[21] There was a girl in our group whose name is Malia (Muh-lee-uh). That's what she told us. And she gets to Kia Aroha and she meets one of the Samoan . . .

JDA: *Wait, wait, wait . . . What do you mean that's what she told you?*

TIFFANI MARIE: That's what she told us. Her name was Malia.

JDA: She wasn't your student?

TIFFANI MARIE: She was our student. This is our student. She said that everybody called her Malia. And we get to Kia Aroha, and this auntie meets her for the first time and she looked at her and asked her name. And my kid says "Malia." Auntie moves on and she's doing her thing and then she references her and she says, Malia (Mal-ē-uh). My kids were like, "Did you hear how she just said your name? And Malia (Mal-ē-uh) says, "Yeah, that's my name." For me, that was it. I was in the back and I don't even think the kids knew I was there yet. But I was so floored that I had already spent almost the entire year with this kid and that someone could look at her and know her in a way . . . you could truly get in trouble with that. People change kids' names all the time, but that woman was right. And Malia gets back to the States and starts correcting people. And then she changes her last name from Frost, which is her colonial last name, to Niuatoa, which was the last name of her people that she hadn't said in years. She changed it on PowerSchool![22]

In one interaction with this Auntie, [it changed] the way in which she started to move . . . and there were certain people and teachers who still called her Malia (Muh-lee-uh). I bring up that example because it's so subtle, but it's so informed. It is informed by so much wisdom that our relationship shifted because I was committed to learn this child's name, and the meaning behind her name; where it comes from. We were like, well, let's do the *sasa*. I don't know if you know the *sasa*, but it's a Samoan drill that they learned from this one trip. And she started leading our kids through it. No. When she learned it, she was remembering. Because it was something that had been suppressed. I think kids really started having tremendous respect for this act of memory. It was welcomed in our space. There was a respect and that's why when another kid came in our room, our kids would say "You're on sacred ground, take your shoes off." So, it did not just inform my relationship with these kids but informed their relationship to the space and to the work that they were doing there.

You know, another kid . . . this is around naming and it feels very important right now in my spirit . . . his parents wanted to take him out of our school because they felt like what we were centering was not going to prepare him for higher ed. *And*, he had a Black girlfriend. So, it was just too much. And she's in our program. These Chinese parents were like, "Nah . . . you messin' stuff up. We came here because we heard about your data and we want our kid to get into college." We were super sad because he basically just came to say goodbye. We had had all these groundbreaking experiences with this kid. A few days later, in my grief, I had remembered a conversation with him where because of that experience with Malia, I wanted to learn more about our kids' names and I wanted to center that in our work. I remember a conversation we had, and this was time outside of the classroom where our kids would drop by and want to share these profound revelations. In our previous cohorts we would be like "Come on, you gotta get to class. You got to go. What are you doing? They about to come for me."

We stopped that for a while and just really started listening to kids. And one of those days, he came in and we were talking about his middle name. His middle name is Kai Jie . . . which means one who returns from war triumphantly and those around him celebrate his return. So, they had already removed him from the school. And I'm sad, super sad, because I had done so much with him. He was just an amazing leader, particularly around masculinity. He just really was loving feminist ideologies and we had done a lot around the anti-Blackness that was very much surrounding him. And then I was reminded of his middle name. And I texted him. And I was like, "Dude, we'll be fine. We'll be fine." And we started talking about it. And there was a lot of "lol" in this text chat. He's in our program this year. He's back with us in our program this year. You don't know the value of what you know without knowing what it is centered in . . . because that was not my focus in the first and second iteration of the program. I don't know most of my kids' middle names. I don't know why they were named what they were named. I was focused on this kid and this name with a P, "present", or an A, "absent" next to it. And we still had great conversations in class about things that I thought were relevant, but it shifted when it was about their health and how those relationships moved was fundamentally different.

JDA: *Wooh. You almost had me leakin' there.*

TIFFANI MARIE: Yeah. And a lot of that. I've done a lot of that. That one . . . I had to take that one out of a few presentations. I had it in there and I couldn't get through it because I genuinely feel the moment I had the revelation about it . . . he'll be back and he'll be fine.

JDA: *How would you describe your responsibility as an educator, and can you give an example of a time when you feel that your practice reflected that responsibility and an example of a time when you feel like it did not?*

TIFFANI MARIE: I realized that this work is so intense that you can't do it well unless you're doing it for yourself. Kids will see right through it. I used to rhetorically say I was responsible to young people, and so much of my responsibility was still upholding the structure of schooling. I genuinely, today, can say that I feel responsible to improving the health of Black children. I know that I feel responsible for creating spaces that do that and perfecting practices that do that. I know that when Black children are well, all children are well.

So, in the past, when I've been more responsible, or felt more accountable, to the school building and its functions, I have asked students to leave my program when I had been embarrassed by them. It was *my* program. We've had some conversations about this in the past; some hard lines that I felt like I had to take, which I wouldn't do today. One of those experiences was with these kids who had this rap group and they did a video that was about running a train on this girl. They did a song and the video they filmed in the classroom. They filmed it in *my* classroom. So, ego took center stage and the approach was "How dare you!" We had all of this . . . the video has to come down. And they were like, "This video had 1,500 hits the first day. There's no way it's coming down." I rhetorically was saying I was responsible to their health and well-being, but in practice it was very much about Tiff's ego and it was about how, if I can be transparent, can I get kids to continue to conform to what I want if this is allowed? This cannot be okay. Kids are watching. I now know that's not true. I now know that kids are very much able to understand that each kid has different needs. I know that now. I did not know that then. It was very manipulative, because years later they said, "when you told us to leave." Because that's what their hearts experienced. And I framed it as if *they* made the choice to leave. I think that's a situation where I still very much saw school and the mechanisms of school as redeemable and alive and valuable. And today, I just wouldn't do that.

Today I would actually see their product—the video and the filming and where they filmed it—as an assessment of my own practice. But I didn't have the humility. I didn't actually have enough people to say, "I hear you that you're hurt and let's think of that as a measurement of what you're actually conveying is OK." So, today, if that were to happen and I truly were responsible to the health and well-being of young people, I would measure that as: *we've* cultivated, collectively, a space where that's okay and *we* (not *they*) have disrespected me, but *we* have so much work to do together because this is a lifelong process.

The thing is, when they were asked to leave, they came around every week and I was like, "Yeah, yeah . . . see." And they took the video down much later, but that happened organically. We still developed a relationship with them. We still opened the door. We still engaged. I still texted them. I still talked to T on the anniversary of his brother's death. I still met with O when he dropped out. But there was a pain, so deep, around that one decision that it altered our relationship forever. I love them. They love me. They came to that group's rites of passage ceremony when they were seniors. But they knew. They knew that my practice was faulty. And their friends who stayed in knew it too. They knew I was a part of them having to choose . . . all of that garbage. That stayed with us.

But today, I have a lot of grief around it. I sit with it. It's not about moving on from it. It's about acknowledging it. I have countless other examples. If we're to be honest, as educators, I have countless examples of being more responsible to the school and its mechanisms than to the children and their health and well-being. Unfortunately. And now it's really just about shifting that score in the count. And I'm really committed to creating and cultivating opportunities where kids are confident that I choose them. They're confident because we are more responsible to them, which means listening to them when they are out of a class and want to come to us. Centering their voices and their desires for what they want for themselves. We had a number of kids who climbed trees. That's just what they do. We have a number of kids who have to move . . . they have to. So being responsible to them, based on who we had in that group, we had to take the desks out of the room. And we had the cool IKEA standing desks . . . I was hot because we spent so much money on that. The desks had to go. It was compromising their health. The following year there had to be all these alterations to the classroom design and culture because we were responsible to *them* and not to these practices and procedures that really would make *us* feel better and prevent us from dealing with our shit.

JDA: *Based on everything you said and also on my own experience, I wonder about that too. Would it [choosing school or program over children] really make you feel better? That's what you tell yourself. But, if you're truly reflective, you realize that it doesn't. But by toxifying the children, which by definition means you've toxified your space, there's no avoiding breathing in that ether. That's the claim, or the statement—that when Black children are well, then we'll all be well.*

TIFFANI MARIE: Yep. It was deep because we had a number of kids who were really with our program. They were with it. It was always our Black children whose bodies were the most honest. It was beyond them. They weren't trying to be . . . it was that their bodies were the most honest.

JDA: *Yeah. And where the body goes, the mind and mouth will follow.*

TIFFANI MARIE: For sure.

JDA: *After eighteen years as an educator, artist, scholar, researcher—a lot of that precedes even your time working with young people—what are your thoughts about the role of education in the pursuit of justice, freedom, and self-determination for Black folks specifically, and non-dominant folks generally?*

TIFFANI MARIE: I mean, it's been a theme throughout this interview. The role of education is to return you to your greater self. I think we all have the ability to do it. I think some of us have done more work to experience it. I've learned that the greatest thing I can do as an educator is to heal myself. I've learned so much about what it means to be your greater self, only because I've done it for myself. And I've been coming to terms with how much has been lost in these years of this pursuit of what we have been calling education that hasn't been that.

What is coming to me is that I've really been passionate about the idea of how we share what we feel, our emotions. I've been into a lot of psychology work lately. What's been interesting is this idea of both our primary and our secondary emotions. Some of the texts that I've been listening to, or reading, talk about how when we're children, in every household, there are acceptable and unacceptable emotions. Acceptable and unacceptable things to feel and to articulate our feelings around. So, for my household, happiness was a very acceptable emotion. Sadness and fear were not and so those are the ones that were corrected very quickly. And of course, if it's gendered, it's exacerbated. What I've been learning in that work is that because so much of that was unacceptable, we never learned how to be in relationship with some of those emotions. What we got good at instead is responding to the secondary emotions that come up because the primary ones were not okay. We've been told that those are not okay. So, when I . . . and I am talking about myself first because I truly feel like so much of this is about the practitioner first and we don't get to say that, and we don't get to do it, talk about it and center it. I've learned how to deal with my primary emotions, and I've been learning more and more how to deal with the moments in my life when I was told that it was not okay to do it because it's been those moments that have informed how I teach and what I see as education or educational.

So, little Tiffani, and so much of my trauma happened when I was like six . . . I have to respond to her today. That informs what I think I'm actually doing in this work. So, when I think about teachers in general, and I just said this and I was super scared to talk about it but we did . . . is that so much of what we think we're doing in our work as it relates to education is we think we are showing up for these children. And really so many of us are showing up for ourselves first. Which is actually okay if we start telling the truth. And a lot of teachers are like, "I think children are the future, or I really love math—I have a heart for it." And under all those really fluffy reasons about why people are doing the work that they're doing, there's trauma. A lot of folks had horrible experiences as children, and they want it to be better for children. A lot of folks, in schools particularly, had no one who looked like them. So, they're like, "I want to be that person for other children." A lot of people even say, "I had this amazing teacher," and then they don't trip off the fact that you remember that one teacher and them being that amazing to you, means that it was really sparse and you didn't have that in other spaces.

So much of our entrance into this work and what we think we're doing . . . the foundation of it is trauma. And, so I just want to be transparent about it. I genuinely believe that I am here to save myself, and in that process, I think, that is education. Then I attempt to model what I'm learning with and for my young people. It's come from the different sections I've been talking about in this interview. The ability to save myself and to live more abundantly has to be intimately connected to both remembering these ways and practices of sustainability that have held me and my people through worlds that have ended prior to this one . . . and showing up for that little Tiffani who experienced extreme harm in a school. And that translated to how I saw myself . . . in me wanting to be that Oprah. In me wanting to be able to take some of that power back. All of that comes from that experience. This act of education is a confrontation of those traumas, but also an extension of my memory beyond that.

So, I do believe that what it means to be a self-determined people is the ability to heal ourselves. And to heal each other. And to not rely on a structure that literally was created for our demise to be the same structure that heals us. It's absurd to me. I believe that healing, actual healing—and I differentiate healing from health . . . I think healing gets us toward homeostasis . . . toward the ability to sit still and connect to the trees, toward the ability to do our Reiki meditation. I think healing gets us there. But I think health and sustained health is about the ability to normatively do those things where they're not compromised on a day-to-day basis, which might have to happen in these maroon spaces.

So, this project—and I don't really use the language of justice because it's complicated for Black people in America—but when we talk about freedom, when we talk about being self-determined, I see my role and what I'm doing in education as saying first is this ability to have the tools, the resources, the consciousness, the understand-ing to save yourself, to heal yourself, to save your own life, and then part of education is to actually move us toward being able to do it sustainably. I feel like we're always under attack. And I don't think it has to be that way. And I think sometimes we're constantly under attack because we keep doing this work.

The last thing I would say is how profound *Song of Solomon* has been to me. Milkman is cool, but it was the character Circe that does it for me. After Pilate and Macon II see their dad shot off of this fence, because he's a successful Black dude, they flee. And this woman, Circe, has a desire to protect them. And she gets them, and she gets them in the house, and she's trying to feed them jam and it just doesn't taste like fresh fruit, so they're thrown off. We later realize that she's hiding them in the house of the people who killed their dad. And I see so many of our practices in the same way, as we keep trying to hide and protect these kids in the house of these murderers of their ancestors. It's not working. So, when I think about education and its connection and correlation to being self-determined, through that memory, through the saving of ourselves,

I think one of the most fundamental things that education does is it makes us make a choice. Because we know we can't do both. You cannot protect children in the house of their parents' murderers. It's not possible. And so I think education, and I won't even say critical education, but education makes that choice to put young people and ourselves in positions where we can consistently reclaim ourselves.

East Oakland Step to College

When I think about my responsibility as an educator, I think about particular students that have graced my life and my classroom with a kind of truth telling that reminded me of my sacred purpose as an educator in our community. When I think about my responsibility, I think about creating classroom climates and cultures that meet the needs of those students; the ones that schools often disregard and discard because the truth of their lives is incredibly inconvenient for institutional practices that frequently treat youth wellness as an afterthought.

For most of my classroom teaching career, I have looped with my students. This is more common in elementary schools than in secondary schools, but essentially looping is when a cohort of students have the same teacher for multiple years. Early in my career, the looping was more organic and informal. At the end of the school year, I would go to the counselor and ask for particular groups of students to be programmed into my class for the following year. I experienced no resistance to these requests because I was asking to keep the students that most of my colleagues preferred to avoid. Eventually, I developed cohort models where I was their high school English teacher for three to four years, taking students all the way through high school graduation.

One such cohort was at my neighborhood high school—the one where my own sons will naturally matriculate. A number of my students were literally my neighbors' children. At the start of our cohort in 2009, it was one of the worst-performing high schools in the state of California. It still is. In our second year of the cohort, Reina, one of our students, shared a story with our class that to this day shapes my understanding about my responsibility as an educator. She was not always so open, though.

In 2009, on the first day of class for the cohort, Reina showed up committed, but not to our cohort. Within minutes of the start of our first class, she started a fistfight with another student in the cohort. We were fortunate that my colleague and co-teacher, along with four of my university students, were there on that day. After we broke up the fight, Reina sat with me in the back of the class and the other student went outside the room with the co-teacher. There was an eerie silence among the other students while I held her hand and her entire body heaved with adrenaline. After several awkward seconds, one of the other students asked, "Can we go over the syllabus now?"

"This *is* the syllabus," I responded indignantly. "You come as you are, and this is where we are right now. Nothing matters more to us."

Reina pushed my hands away and spoke loudly enough for the class to hear, "Go ahead, send me to the principal."

"Huh?"

"Send me to the principal. You're a teacher. You have to. Send me to the principal."

"I am a teacher. I am also your Tío, whether you know that or not. We don't send people to the principal. This is a community, and we handle our own."

After several minutes of insistence that as a teacher I was *required* to send her to school authorities, Reina accepted that something different was going to happen in our space. She had little to say in that moment, but this event began a journey together that, with fits and spurts, led to a moment that profoundly reminded me about my responsibility as an educator.

During Reina's tenth-grade year, over a year after that first day's fight, she stood in front of our class and shared the following poem that she wrote as part of the culminating performance of her critical autoethnography project:[23]

My poem is called "More scars than birthdays"

If I had a gun
Pointed to my head
And my life
Flashed before my eyes
I would see
The times
I would smoke
With ma cousins
Drinking,
Smacking,
Doing powder
Till I knew
I was too gone
Cheating on my boyfriend
With my ex
Because he would tell me
He still loved me
Lyin to the people I love
Hurtin the people
That care about me most
And then
I would see the reason why
I would see a little girl . . .

At this point in the performance of the poem, Reina began to cry. She choked on her words and stood frozen, staring at her poem, in front of a class full of her fifteen- and sixteen-year-old peers. One of my very first students from Oakland, who had become a social studies teacher in Oakland and joined this cohort as a teaching fellow while working on his PhD, shouted out "You can do it!" Then, one of her fellow students shouted out "We're with you!" as Reina sobbed and her chest heaved. We waited. Our silence only broken by Reina's sobs. And then, she looked up from her paper and continued:

I would see a little girl
Getting raped
At the age of four years old
She didn't know what to do
Or who to talk to,
She was so afraid
That she would cry
And not tell anybody
She stayed silent
I would see
Four years passing by
Rape after rape
After rape
I would see an 8 year old girl
With more scars
Than birthdays
I would see
A 13 year old girl
Getting raped
By her first real boyfriend
I would see a girl
Who didn't know
How to love herself
I would see . . . me

And if I had a gun
Pointed to my head [*sobbing again*],
And I had minutes
Left to live
I would tell that little girl
It's okay to tell your mom,
It's safe to cry,
Go through your pain
So you can heal,
Drugs will not
Heal your pain
Will not block it out.
Love yourself,
One day:
Trust somebody,
Love somebody,
Let yourself be loved . . .
If I had a gun pointed
At my head
I would cry
And tell 15 year old me
"I love you,
Don't regret your mistakes"
Because I've learned
That my mistakes
Are the lessons
I needed to learn
So I could
Create a better future.[24]

With Reina's face peeking out from behind her poem, the class erupted with applause and cheers.

She had been carrying that story since she was four years old. She went through kindergarten, first grade, second, third, fourth, fifth, sixth, seventh, eighth, and our ninth-grade class before the space was created where she felt she could share that story. Of *course* that's the child who starts a fight on the first day of class. That's not the question at issue. The question is, *When are we going to change the way that we respond to that child?* Because when we change the way we respond to the child, the space is opened up for the child to show up fully and truly, with all of their woundedness and all of their desire for the commitment to care that makes healing possible for them. How do we meet our responsibility to create educational environments where a child can bring *that* truth to her teenage peers without fear of cyberbullying? Without fear of gossip spreading through the hallways? How do we meet our responsibility to create educational environments where a child can bring *that* truth to her teenage peers and be fully held by her community in that moment of vulnerability? Answers to those questions establish the foundation of the responsibility that we are to stand on as educators. Full stop.

That *is* rigor. The young people in our classroom community held Reina like that because they were up next and they too were bringing stories that would require holding from the community. As long as we keep talking about academic rigor and social justice as if they are somehow separate, we are doing neither. There is no rigor without relationships, relevance, and our responsibility to social justice. And there is no social justice without rigor. Until our schools model this fact, our nation certainly will not.

---— CHAPTER 7 ———

SCHOOLING OR EDUCATION

Which One Will We Choose?

Let's begin by saying that we are living through a very dangerous
time. . . . We are in a revolutionary situation, no matter how
unpopular that word has become in this country. The society in
which we live is desperately menaced . . . from within. To any
citizen of this country who figures himself as responsible—and
particularly those of you who deal with the minds and hearts of
young people—must be prepared to "go for broke." Or to put it
another way, you must understand that in the attempt to correct
so many generations of bad faith and cruelty, when it is operating
not only in the classroom but in society, you will meet the most
fantastic, the most brutal, and the most determined resistance.
There is no point in pretending that this won't happen.

                                        —James Baldwin, "A Talk to Teachers"

This concluding chapter revisits the basic premise of this book,
which is that we are going to have to choose between tinkering
with our current model of an equal education system or make the
hard pivot toward an equitable one. Valenzuela has described this as

a choice between schooling children and educating them. Schooling is the process by which you institutionalize children to, more or less, accept their position in life. It is a model of social reproduction that produces the aesthetic of care without ever really committing to the much harder work of creating an environment of authentic care.[1] Education is the process where young people's infinite capacity to dream is nurtured such that they come to understand their capability to shape their own lives and their responsibility to do so in a way that genuinely wrestles with the morality and ethics necessary for the growth of a democracy committed to wellness, justice, and equitable outcomes for all its people. The chapter focuses on recommendations for six groups that will be central to successfully making this change: funders, policy makers, researchers, teacher educators, educational leaders, and teachers.

Many years ago, one of my elders shared a story with me that appropriately frames the choice before us in this work. It is the story of a little boy who was playing in the front yard of his Abuelita's home. He came charging into the house and ran up to his Abuelita and said "Abuelita, I feel like there is a war going on inside my head."

"There is, mijo," Abuelita responded.

"Who's fighting Abuelita?"

"The two wolves."

"Who are the two wolves?"

"Ahh . . . one wolf is rage, avarice, selfishness, greed, violence," Abuelita said.

"Who is the other wolf?" the boy wondered aloud.

"The other wolf is love, joy, family, community, empathy."

The boy thought for a moment. "Who wins, Abuelita?"

The grandmother gave a wry smile and answered, "The one you feed."

For many years, I shared this story as a way to end my lectures on the topics covered in this book. I used the story as a way to make it clear that the day-to-day disconnections that happen for children at school are primarily attributable to adult decisions. The story works to that end for storytellers such as myself because it paints a very clean and clear binary. It is a quintessentially American allegory. Manicheanism at its best, with all the good on one side and all the bad on the other.

To some degree, I still believe that the story works to illustrate pivotal choices we make in our lives about how we will respond in moments when those around us are presenting in ways that trigger that first wolf. My thinking about this was changed a bit by an Indigenous scholar who attended one of my talks. Some days after my time in their community, he emailed me and reminded me that the first wolf is not to be expunged or overcome. Rather, the two wolves, together, are never going away. They comprise our full humanity. The goal should not be to eliminate the more painful side of our two wolves (for we cannot), but to understand those emotions and balance them out with the truths of their counterparts.

This teaching was repeated for me just a few weeks ago when I was conducting the interview with Yaa Tiffani Marie that is transcribed in chapter 6. In our conversation, she reminded me about households where parents create expectations about emotions that are encouraged (happiness, joy, wonder) and emotions that are discouraged (sadness, anger, frustration). These expectations are sometimes conveyed subtly and sometimes not so subtly. We teach our children through our responses to their authentic emotions (the two wolves) that one wolf is desirable and one wolf is troublesome. I have been this parent. I have been this teacher. I have tried to talk my sons and my students out of their more painful emotions in an effort to assure myself that I am doing a good job. I try my best to no longer do that with children or adults. Instead, I attempt to be an empathic witness to their feelings, appreciating them as part of our journey together. In the most painful moments, where I have attempted to convince my students and my own children that it will be better on the other side, I have unwittingly (ignorantly) denied that the "bad" wolf is the right wolf in that moment. Those feelings are not only legitimate, they are real and righteous. We can never be well if we do not avail ourselves of the entire emotional spectrum, and our children cannot be well if we do not create environments that encourage the same. The wolf that we choose to feed is important, but the other wolf is not going away because it is just as much a part of our humanity.

ROLE RECOMMENDATIONS

Funders

The very idea that "funders" exist is a problem. Educational innovation has a major dilemma in that the most prominent supporters of innovation do not support innovation at all. Anand Giridharadas's book, *Winners Take All*, is but one example of the increasing feeling that the superrich (and mostly white) aristocracy have decided to use philanthropy to express their not-so-well concealed sentiment that they know what is best for communities with whom they have virtually no meaningful contact.[2]

We should not be shocked, stunned, or amazed at the fact that the nation's educational agenda is so deeply and profoundly influenced by people who do not have an ounce of experience at educating children (other than, perhaps, their own). As this book has clearly laid out, the history of the primary influencers of public schools is deeply problematic. From the outset, the public school project has been guided by wealthy (mostly white) people who entitled themselves to define creativity, ingenuity, and valid measures of achievement for the nation's most vulnerable youth and the schools they attend.

Were funders to care to redirect this trend, they would first need to acknowledge their complicity in it. Then, they would need to muster the courage and commitment to radically reorganize their portfolios to support the work of educators, organizations, and scholars whose work has provided meaningful challenges and alternatives to the failed public school project. This support cannot sit in some "special interest" or "diversity" portion of the funder's strategic plan. Rather, it must sit at the center of the strategic plan and it must be a long-term commitment that reckons with the fact that this shift is an effort to undo a centuries-long project of under-education and miseducation.

This shift would require some serious soul-searching on the part of the nation's superrich and those who have chosen to carry out the project of redistributing marginal percentages of their ill-begotten gains to the very communities that paid the steepest price for them to garner all that wealth in the first place. That is a complex sentence to represent a sick and twisted system of aristocratic false generosity that has mostly been developed to alleviate the unsettled consciences of crooks in castles. There is nothing about the current concept of philanthropy that poses any real disruptive threat to the systems of inequity that all but guarantee that the philanthropists will maintain their wealth and those they are "helping" will remain observers of that wealth from deep in the margins of our society. Were I wrong here—and I hope that one day I am—then philanthropists would have to be far more comfortable with regular proximity to those whose pain they hope to help to relieve. They would have to trust that what is best for those communities should be defined only by those communities and that those things may very well undermine truths that the super elite hold most dear to their hearts. They would also need to embrace communities being self-determining of their own metrics of success and progress, rather than asserting that their wealth status is somehow an indicator that they know best how to measure progress in the very communities they have devastated through their excessive accumulation of wealth. Philanthropists would also have to get comfortable with the reality that were they to truly redistribute their wealth (nothing in the current funding world suggests that there is a serious agenda to do this) it would radically alter their concept of philanthropy, their ability to maintain their wealth and power, and their own children's futures. It would also mean that more people and more communities, including themselves and their children, would be more well.

Policy Makers

This group has a particularly challenging task for two reasons. First, educational policy has too often been framed in ways that lead to overly deterministic policies that have been far too sweeping at every level. Secondly, policy makers have historically not had sufficient proximity to the pain they are attempting to resolve. This does not make them bad people; it just makes them ignorant. The result has been policies that are based on a desire to solve problems that is largely based on the worldview of the privileged with little to no inquiry and input from the very people who are most in need of policy change that supports them. At best, these sorts of policies temporarily relieve the systems of suffering, but they never address the root causes that guarantee that that suffering returns over and over again. The sensibility driving these two approaches is one that presumes that all students need and deserve the same thing, a belief that is directly at odds with the principles of community responsiveness and equity discussed in this book.

For policy makers to support community responsiveness and equity, they would need to be committed to spending significantly more time in the nation's most vulnerable and wounded communities. And they would need to see the residents of those communities as capable of designing better solutions for their challenges than the policy makers themselves. In addition, they would need to embrace the idea that policy is most likely to have impact when it supports communities to be self-determining of their definitions of wellness and success and in control of their own resources to solve their own challenges to achieve those things.

Researchers

With rare exceptions, educational research has left much to be desired. I could wax poetic on the various reasons that educational research (including my own) has had minimal impact on mainstream school culture and practices, but this section is more about what educational researchers might do differently to have a more meaningful impact.

Education is a unique enterprise, one that is a far cry from controlled laboratories or the county general hospital. Educators interact with their students almost every day for nine months each year. The frequency of interactions between teachers and students significantly differentiates education interventions from the other enterprises that conventional thinking suggests are worth modeling ourselves after. The traditional educational discourse and research methodology, which focuses on things and ideas rather than people and material conditions, has largely resulted in an educational research paradigm that seeks to find what David Tyack dubbed the "one best system."[3] For the most vulnerable children in particular, this effort to create cookie-cutter reform models has meant decades of educational, social, and economic stagnation and marginalization.

Research agendas that centralize care and wellness emphasize reciprocal relationships with schools, leading to deeper commitments by researchers to the school's and the community's welfare. This kind of educational research respects that each school's unique set of stakeholders and material conditions requires a research methodology that recognizes these differences. Rather than aiming to develop a model that can be laid on top of any school, this educational research approach focuses on forming relationships that pay attention to the special needs of a particular school. This focus on relationships translates into a greater emphasis on producing real change in the schools where the research is taking place.

An approach to educational research that emphasizes care and wellness must, by definition, be community responsive. Some have called this "action research" and described it as an intervention for "emancipatory change": "In stark contrast to 'policy studies,' whose aim is to provide 'useful,' expert knowledge for institutional planning, the core of critical action research involves its participatory and communally discursive structure and the cycle of action and reflection it initiates. The knowledge enabled through such reflexive and shared study leads not to bureaucratic directives, but, more important, to the possibility for emancipatory change."[4]

The value of this type of community responsive research is its focus on developing and sustaining the community's power to be self-determining agents of meaningful, sustainable change. The direct aim of this type of research agenda is to positively impact the material conditions of those involved with the study; it is an approach to research that gives more than it receives. By focusing more directly on improving the immediate circumstances, it de-emphasizes the traditional method of searching for empirical truths that can be implemented on a large scale. Instead, it taps into the long history of indigenous research and knowledge creation in communities that dominant research paradigms often treat as devoid of these practices.[5] This way, if and when researchers leave, they leave behind an increased sense of hope and promise, one that is directly tied to the individual actors sense of themselves as capable change agents. Beyond a heightened awareness of the capacity to change, this kind of research also leaves behind a more refined set of tools that can be used and reused to continually improve the conditions that are most in need of attention. This is particularly unique, because dominant culture research methods isolate tools in the hands of the researchers, and so when the researchers leave, so does the sense that the tools to do research have left with them.

Community-responsive research agendas that are committed to collaboration with participants as colleagues rather than subjects can result in richer studies. This approach reduces dependency-based colonial models of knowledge production that have historically reproduced the status quo. By inserting multiple voices into the conversation, the process of identifying problems and researching solutions becomes more democratic. As well, this research program provides a grounded, structured form for individual and structural reflexivity that can serve as a mechanism for ongoing feedback and adaptation as new and different issues arise that need the attention of research. Perhaps most importantly, it recognizes the complexity of each individual set of conditions and encourages a sensibility of self-determination in the form of local agency and control for developing solutions for local problems. This is not to say that sites cannot learn from the research of others; this is not a subtractive model or a zero-sum game. Instead, this is an additive model of educational research, one that suggests that research designed to create sweeping policy amendments will not be sufficient to bring about the local attention to change that is necessary in institutions like schools. What is necessary is a localized research that supports dynamic and flexible policy change that gives communities the autonomy and right to be self-determining in the education of their children.

Teacher Educators

Freire argued that the primary purpose of education should be to inscribe hope in the lives of the students. He described hope as an "ontological need," especially in the lives and the pedagogy of educators working in communities where forms of social misery seem to have taken up permanent residence.[6] Hope has always been a theme in the lives and movements of the poor and dispossessed in this country. During the Civil Rights Era, as well as other key historical moments of social change, the nation's hope connected moral outrage to action aimed at resolving undeserved suffering. Educators cannot simply call an end to the conditions of inequality in our society. However, we can develop pedagogy that is responsive to those conditions *and* academically rigorous, such that we begin to rebuild the critical hope that has been worn down in these communities. Such educators deliver us from false hope by teaching in ways that connect the moral outrage of young people to actions that relieve the undeserved suffering in their communities. The spread of this kind of educational practice in our schools adds to the hopefulness because it develops transgenerational capacity for long-term sustainable critical hope in communities.

If teacher education is going to do its part, our field will need to make changes in three key areas: recruitment, curriculum and instruction, and mentoring.[7]

RETHINKING RECRUITMENT. Teacher education continues to fail to recruit and attract students of color, particularly candidates from the racial groups that struggle the most in our schools (Indigenous, Black, Latinx, and Pacific Islander). Oddly enough, this "recruiting" challenge (especially for Black, Latinx, and Pacific Islander students) does not seem to present itself to athletic programs on college and university campuses. Teacher education would do well to learn from sports programs that have successfully recruited from communities of color for decades. This will require them to get into schools, as early as elementary school, to start forming relationships with young people, families, and educators, encouraging and incentivizing their matriculation into teaching. Programs such as Clemson University's Call Me Mister or San Francisco State University's Pin@y Educational Partnerships (PEP) are steps in the right direction.

In addition to more aggressive recruitment of teacher candidates who more closely represent the racial and social background of urban students, schools of education must also pay greater attention to screening applicants for a commitment to supporting the most wounded and vulnerable youth. This allows for targeted recruitment of candidates with that specific purpose for joining the profession and more focused allocation of resources to develop that purpose. Several programs around the country are attempting to make this commitment, the most prominent of which may be UCLA's Center X, and this is also a move in the right direction.

CURRICULUM AND INSTRUCTION. It is impossible to teach someone how to teach in a university classroom. As teacher educators, we should be more honest with our students about this fact. From the university classroom, we can give teacher candidates three things: (1) cutting-edge theory and research, (2) a critical and supportive community of peers and mentors, and (3) a preliminary credential. To do these most effectively, teacher educators should have firsthand knowledge of the conditions in the schools where they are sending students *and* the practices that work there. They should also be able to model that kind of effective practice themselves. On this point, teacher education would do well to change its faculty recruitment criteria by prioritizing context-specific, ongoing, field-based successful practice as a primary requisite for teaching future teachers. This would require collaborating with doctoral programs and local school districts to actively recruit faculty candidates with these qualifications.[8]

If we grow the number of teacher educators who are active in K–12 classrooms, the curriculum in teacher education will change just based on the faculty's practical experience in the field. However, we should also make an explicit effort to include relevant, cutting-edge research that raises understanding of the conditions to which classroom pedagogy must respond. These changes can be coupled with forums with righteous scholars and practitioners from an array of other disciplines, including public health, medicine, child services, immigration advocacy, and law. Finally, the curriculum should involve regular instruction from, and discussions with, community members, students, parents, and effective teachers who come from the schools and communities where these teachers in training are headed.

FROM MENTORING TO APPRENTICESHIP. Teacher education should also move toward an apprenticeship model where future teachers apprentice under highly skilled pedagogues for multiple years before being allowed to direct their own classroom. To accomplish this, each program will first need to develop rigorous criteria for selecting exceptional teachers to become mentors. This effort can proceed using a two-pronged approach: a community-nomination model;[9] and a teacher-quality index.[10] If my previous advice is followed to recruit potential teachers earlier, then these relationships are more likely to take the form of actual apprenticeships, evolving over multiple years. The relationship would ideally begin in a student's first or second university year and continue throughout their career. The premier program would allow teacher candidates and mentors to select each other, forming a more natural and invested start to their relationship. The limited number of skilled and experienced pedagogues will require careful planning such that cohorts of apprentices progress through different levels with their mentor (as we see in the trades, law, business, medicine, and the martial arts).

The upsides of an apprenticeship model are numerous. First, it creates a steady inflow of undergraduates with commitment as well as cultural and experiential alignment—provided that the aforementioned recruitment strategy is followed. I have seen these kinds of intentional teacher pipelines create a consistency and staying power among teachers that result in extensive years of service in the highest need schools.

As well, if university credential programs use instructional methods that are inclusive of students' apprenticeship experiences, it creates the opportunity for applied discussions of course readings and fertile ground for meaningful problem-solving exercises and sharing of firsthand experiences. Apprenticeship models are also more likely to create formal and lasting partnerships between teacher education programs and the strongest teachers in the area, developing a deep resource pool for supporting better research and practice. Finally, this approach stands to cultivate meaningful mentorship relationships between early-career and veteran teachers in the community—something sorely lacking that contributes greatly to high rates of early-career teacher turnover.[11]

Educational Leaders

Over the past six years, I have come to understand just how challenging—dare I say, absurd?—the roles of school and system leaders are. I have immense respect for those who do it well. Teachers would do well to spend a day shadowing a community-responsive educational leader. I know that as a teacher, I really did not have a good handle (at all) on the work that my principals were doing each day. This too often led me to be dismissive of the importance and complexity of their work.

In the same breath, I have encountered far too many school leaders who think that leadership means dictating. In so doing, they fail to honor the challenge and toll paid by their community-responsive colleagues and they create an environment that is not healthy for teachers, children, or families. The most effective leaders I have encountered are committed to being servant-leaders, a concept often attributed to Greenleaf, although I was first introduced to this concept in Woodson's *The Mis-Education of the Negro*, where he writes:

"The real servant of the people must live among them, think with them, feel for them, and die for them."[12] The servant-leader knows that their leadership is best displayed through service to the staff, children, and families and that for that service to be true and meaningful they must be community responsive. They must keep their finger on the pulse of the community with no task beneath them and the focus where it belongs—on those who have the least.

One of the most important lessons I have come to learn as an educational leader is that the same things that worked with children in my classroom are the same things that work with adults. This continues to be a profoundly challenging principle for me to uphold, but I believe it to be fundamentally true. As depicted in my writing here and across the years, my commitment to children in my life has always been to make sure they knew they could always count on my commitment to build spaces and relationships where they were seen, heard, and loved. As imperfect as those spaces always were, there was a deep and relentless commitment on my part to keep listening, to keep iterating, and to be in their lives forever.

This always came easily to me as a teacher; maybe because I did not experience that kind of commitment from most of my teachers. So, as Dr. Patrick Camangian told me once about his classroom practice: "I wanted to become the teacher that I never had." I raged against the apathetic and apologist culture that had set in with so many of my teaching colleagues. The kind of culture that was permissive of my rationalizing the times when I came up short with my students: "You just can't reach them all." Well, maybe that statement is true. What is also certainly true is that I could sure as hell try to reach everyone because that is what I signed up to do. And if I was going to insist that my students be "relentless and never ever give up" (see "The Definite Dozen" in my book *What a Coach Can Teach a Teacher*), then I'd best model that same kind of commitment toward them.[13]

When I look at my students, I see the responsibility assigned to me by my ancestors. I see the beauty of innocence, joy, and unrealized potential that is just waiting to be embraced and drawn out. When I started working with adults as an educational leader, I struggled to transfer that sensibility. I saw grown folks, many of whom had advanced degrees, and all of whom were being paid to do the work. The community-responsive pedagogue was subsumed by title and privilege, and I too often forgot that what everyone wants, child or adult, is to be seen, heard, and loved. I just have not met very many people in our profession who want to fail with children. Yet and still, so many are doing just that with incredibly high frequency and consistency. The work of the leader, like the work of the teacher, is to serve those whom we have been called to lead, and we can do that best by using the same kind of community-responsive pedagogy that works with young people in our classrooms.

Educational leaders would do well to remind themselves, and their teachers, why they got into this work in the first place. One of the first things that is taken from us as teachers is our right to dream. We are quickly conditioned (and often rewarded) for compliance and consent, even when those things are wildly at odds with the purpose that brought us to the work. While that purpose, particularly as it relates to teachers coming in with a colonial mentality, is not always worthy of preservation, the intent—with some re-education—often is. This is to say that so many of us come into the work with the purpose and intent to support young people to pursue their dreams and, in fairly quick order, end up willing participants in a set of actions and activities that actually undermine that purpose. One of the most important things that educational leaders can do is to license their teachers to dream again. It should be an annual exercise for educators to revisit the dreams that brought them into the work. Educators who do not dream cannot possibly support young people to dream.

Part and parcel of this commitment to encouraging and empowering teachers to dream again is to trust them as partners in the decision-making processes of a school. The servant-leadership philosophy demands that leaders embrace their responsibility to create collaborative and shared decision-making structures. This is not foreign to a community-responsive pedagogy and it returns us to my earlier point that as teachers, we need the same things our students need. They need us to trust and believe that they know what is best for them to serve our children well. Good leaders are humble enough to realize that fact and also reflective enough to know that the systems where we do our work are designed to discard noncompliant adults and children, just the same.

This is not to say that all the adults who show up to our schools are equivalently committed to the well-being of children. I do not believe that for a second. I do believe, however, that educational leaders often struggle to recognize talent and potential because they are more interested in compliance than commitment. Our best educational leaders are servant-leaders and they are servant-leaders because they are down among the people and committed to the same principled and purposeful compass that defined their best moments as teachers.

Teachers

There is probably no role more important for a successful pivot toward equity than the teacher. As teachers, we cannot wait for permission to do what is right for young people. For certain, the support of policy and leadership at all levels can make equitable work easier to carry out. However, when you have been teaching as long as I have, you know that policy and leadership are, at best, unpredictable and inconsistent. Neither of those levers of change should prevent us from a steadfast commitment to shifting and growing our craft. This is what it means to own our responsibility for the spaces where we do have some modicum of control.

In those times when we are supported to do equity work, we have to push harder and test edges that in less permissive environments we might not otherwise be able to access. In more repressive times, our efforts may need to be more clandestine, but they should be no less intense and purposeful. A commitment to racial and social justice will fall in and out of favor in the rhetorical promises made by power. Educators who only stand watch for justice when the risks are minimal teach our children that equity is not something we fight for, it is something conceded to our communities whenever power deems it necessary and appropriate. Educators who are unwavering in their responsibility to stand by the side of the most vulnerable and wounded ones teach our children that equity is not a program, it is not a policy, and it is not the responsibility of an equity office or an equity officer. Equity is justice and, as is so often said, a threat to justice anywhere is a threat to justice everywhere. Everyone is an equity officer, or no one is an equity officer.

A teacher's responsibility is most obviously reflected in their pedagogy. Pedagogy (particularly equity-based pedagogy), defined as what we teach, how we teach, and why we teach, has been a topic of significant interest for critical scholars since the early twentieth century (if not earlier).[14] In the last several years, there has been a growing interest in Ethnic Studies curriculum and pedagogy.[15] To talk about pedagogy and curriculum as two separate things is a mistake that we must not make—the two are inseparable. As teachers seek to meet their responsibility to children, family, communities, and ancestors, they would do well to engage themselves in the Ethnic Studies movement that is taking shape around the country. There are, however, any number of worrying elements about the expanding adoption of Ethnic Studies in K–12 systems, not the least of which is the total lack of training and expertise among existing teachers to honor the purposeful traditions of Ethnic Studies. Add to this the absence of meaningful pipelines into teaching for students of color with an Ethnic Studies background, and the threats to the sustainability to the K–12 Ethnic Studies movement are quite real. Nevertheless, for educators reading this book, Ethnic Studies pedagogy holds tremendous promise as a site of teacher learning, growth, and collaboration to meet the challenges laid out in this book.

Essential for these changes to happen is that teachers are supported in and committed to being collaborative. For far too long, our profession has been incredibly isolating for teachers. This professional isolation is consistently one of the leading causes for early-career teachers leaving the profession altogether. While collaborating with colleagues, and even team teaching, are certainly much easier when supported by school leaders, teachers should not wait for the institution for validation. Seeking out organizations that support the kind of pedagogy discussed herein, such as those mentioned in chapter 6, might seem like just another thing being added to a teacher's plate. But I can assure you that my collaborative relationships with colleagues is at the top of my list of reasons for staying in schools as long as I have. The energy a teacher will spend seeking out and maintaining meaningful collaborative relationships will have immeasurable returns on their practice and their own well-being. This energy is going to be spent one way or the other, and if it is not spent in collaboration, it will be spent on simply surviving the soul-crushing experience of attempting to do this work in isolation. We will do this together or it will not be done.

CHAPTER 1

1. Diane Ravitch, *The Death and Life of the Great American School System* (New York: Basic Books, 2010).
2. David Tyack and Larry Cuban, *Tinkering Toward Utopia* (Boston: Harvard University Press, 1997).
3. Joel Spring, *American Education: An Introduction to Social and Political Aspects* (New York: Longman, 1989); Joel Spring, *The American School: From the Puritans to No Child Left Behind* (New York: McGraw-Hill, 2008); Ira Katznelson and Margaret Weir, *Schooling for All* (New York: Basic Books, 1985); William H. Watkins, *The White Architects of Black Education* (New York: Teachers College Press, 2001).
4. Spring, *The American School.*
5. *Oxford English Dictionary*, s.v. "equality," https://www-oed-com.jpllnet.sfsu.edu /view/Entry/63702?redirectedFrom=equality#eid.
6. John Dewey, *The Child and the Curriculum* (Chicago: University of Chicago Press, 1902).
7. Abraham Maslow, "A Theory of Human Motivation," *Psychological Review* 50 (1943): 370–96.
8. Brown v. Board of Education of Topeka, 347 U.S. 483 (1954); *Mendez v. Westminster,* 161 F.2d 774 (9th Cir. 1947).
9. Plessy v. Ferguson, 163 U.S. 537 (1896).
10. Steve Luxenberg, *Separate: The Story of* Plessy v. Ferguson, *and America's Journey from Slavery to Segregation* (New York: W. W. Norton, 2019), xviii.
11. *Madeline Will, "Thousands of Black Educators Lost Jobs After Brown v. Board," Education Week 38, June 5, 2019, p. 17.*
12. Watkins, *White Architects of Black Education*, 1.
13. Harry Briggs Jr. et al. v. R. W. Elliott, Chairman, et al. 342 U.S. 350 (1952), dissenting opinion by Waties Waring.
14. Briggs v. Elliot, 76–77.
15. Plessy v. Ferguson.
16. Gary Orfield et al., *Harming Our Common Future: America's Segregated Schools 65 Years after Brown* (UCLA Civil Rights Project, 2019), 1.
17. Orfield et al., *Harming Our Common Future.*
18. Jeffrey Goldberg, "The Surprising Consequences of Brown v. Board of Ed," *The Atlantic*, December 1, 2010.

19. Martha Minow, *In Brown's Wake: Legacies of America's Educational Landmark* (Oxford: Oxford University Press, 2012).
20. Kris Gutiérrez, "White Innocence: A Framework and Methodology for Rethinking Educational Discourse and Inquiry," *International Journal of Learning* 12 (2006): 1–11.
21. Goldberg, "Brown v. Board of Ed."
22. Goldberg.
23. Goldberg.
24. Michelle Alexander, *The New Jim Crow* (New York: The New Press, 2012).
25. Goldberg, "Brown v. Board of Ed.," 3.
26. Vanessa Siddle Walker, *The Lost Education of Horace Tate: Uncovering the Hidden Heroes Who Fought for Justice in Schools* (New York: The New Press, 2018).
27. Leslie T. Fenwick, quoted in Will, *"Thousands of Black Educators Lost Jobs,"* 3–4.
28. Will, *"Thousands of Black Educators Lost Jobs"*; Thomas S. Dee, "Teachers, Race and Student Achievement in a Randomized Experiment," *Review of Economics and Statistics* 86, no. 1 (2004): 195–210; Thomas S. Dee, "A Teacher Like Me: Does Race, Ethnicity, or Gender Matter?," *American Economic Review* 95, no. 2 (2005): 158–65.
29. Seth Gershenson et al., "The Long-Run Impacts of Same-Race Teachers," *Institution of Labor Economics* Discussion Paper Series, IZA DP No. 10630 (2017): 1–62.
30. Gershenson et al., "The Long-Run Impacts," 1.
31. Gershenson, 2–3.
32. Gershenson, 4.
33. Martin Luther King, Jr., "I Have a Dream" (speech, Washington, DC, August 28, 1963).
34. Goldberg, "Brown v. Board of Ed," 1–2.
35. *Unnatural Causes*, directed by Llewellyn Smith, California Newsreel, 2008, https://www.pbs.org/unnaturalcauses/about_the_series.htm; Jennifer L. Eberhardt, *Biased* (New York: Viking Press, 2019); Heather McGhee, *The Sum of Us* (New York: One World, 2021).
36. *Oxford English Dictionary*, s.v. "equity," https://www-oed-com.jpllnet.sfsu.edu/view/Entry/63838?redirectedFrom=equity#eid.

CHAPTER 2

1. Anthony *Bryk* et al., *Learning to Improve: How America's Schools Can Get Better at Getting Better* (Cambridge, MA: Harvard Education Press, *2015*).
2. *Unnatural Causes*, directed by Llewellyn Smith, California Newsreel, 2008, https://www.pbs.org/unnaturalcauses/about_the_series.htm.
3. America's Promise Alliance, "Grad Nation Report Says U.S. on Track to Reach 90 Percent High School Graduation Rate by 2020", CISION PR Newswire, May 12, 2015, https://www.prnewswire.com/news-releases/grad-nation-report-says-us-on-track-to-reach-90-percent-high-school-graduation-rate-by-2020-300081602.html.
4. "Global Wealth Inequality," Inequality.org, https://inequality.org/facts/global-inequality/#us-wealth-concentration.
5. "Global Wealth Inequality."
6. Robert Reich, *Beyond Outrage* (New York: Vintage, 2012); Robert Reich, *Aftershock: The Next Economy and America's Future* (New York: Vintage, 2013).

7. Robert Reich, quoted in *Inequality for All*, directed by Jacob Kornbluth, documentary film, IMDb Productions, 2013.
8. Center on Budget and Policy Priorities, "Income Gains at the Top Dwarf Those of Low and Middle Income Households," CBPP.org, https://www.cbpp.org/income -gains-at-the-top-dwarf-those-of-low-and-middle-income-households-6.
9. Vince Beiser, "Debt to Society" (special report), July 10, 2001, *Mother Jones*, http:// vincebeiser.com/debt-to-society/prisons_download/atlas.html.
10. Beiser, "Debt to Society."
11. Christopher Ingraham, "The States That Spend More Money on Prisoners than College Students," *Washington Post*, July 7, 2016, https://www.washingtonpost.com /news/wonk/wp/2016/07/07/the-states-that-spend-more-money-on-prisoners-than -college-students/.
12. The characterization of spending patterns as a "zero-sum game" is from Heather McGhee, *The Sum of Us* (New York: One World, 2021).
13. John King, quoted in Ingraham, "States That Spend More Money on Prisoners than College Students," 1.
14. McGhee, *The Sum of Us*.
15. "About Us," Vision of Humanity website, https://www.visionofhumanity.org/about/
16. Bryan Stevenson, "Bryan Stevenson of Equal Justice Initiative Speaks at Google" (lecture, Google Campus, Mountain View, CA, February 25, 2016), https://www .youtube.com/watch?v=sWWyT8iQU3M&ab_channel=Google.
17. Community-responsive pedagogy (CRP) advances the work of critical pedagogy and culturally responsive pedagogy by centralizing a community's context in the education of children and youth. It is an equity-centered approach to education that is responsive to the material conditions that are particular to a student's lived experience in a community and the histories that created that experience. The goal of CRP is to use education as a vehicle for liberation through the awakening of students' critical consciousness that leads to actions that promote wellness through racial and social justice in their personal lives, families, and communities and in our world. Community-responsive leaders and educators transform climates, cultures, and curriculum to prioritize youth wellness through a focus on three domains of pedagogical practice: relationships, relevance, and responsibility; see Allyson Tintiangco-Cubales nd Jeff Duncan-Andrade, "Still Fighting for Ethnic Studies: The Origins, Practices, and Potential of Community Responsive Pedagogy," *Teachers College Record* 123, 13 (2021): 1–28.
18. James Baldwin, *Nobody Knows My Name* (London: Vintage Press, 2002), 96.
19. James Garbarino, *Raising Children in a Socially Toxic Environment* (San Francisco: Jossey-Bass, 1995); Shawn Ginwright, *Black Youth Rising* (New York: Teachers College Press, 2009); Shawn Ginwright, *Hope and Healing in Urban Education* (New York: Routledge Press, 2015).
20. *Unnatural Causes.*
21. Ginwright, *Black Youth Rising.*
22. Jeff Duncan-Andrade, "Note to Educators: Hope Required When Growing Roses in Concrete," *Harvard Education Review* 79 no. 2 (2009): 1–13.
23. Ginwright, *Black Youth Rising;* Ginwright, *Hope and Healing;* Duncan-Andrade, "Note to Educators"; David Philoxene, "'Can You Feel Me . . .': The Sociospatial

Logics and Ghost-Map of Black and Urban Youth Navigating Urban Violence" (PhD diss., University of California, Berkeley, 2021).

24. *Unnatural Causes.*

25. Duncan-Andrade, "Note to Educators"; Tiffani Marie Johnson, "Artelia Green's and Olivia Williams' Legacy: A Study on the Pedagogical Practices that Improve Health for Black Children" (PhD diss., University of California, Berkeley, 2020); Angela Valenzuela, *Subtractive Schooling: U.S.-Mexican Youth and the Politics of Caring* (Albany: State University of New York Press, 1999); *Unnatural Causes*; Garbarino, *Raising Children*; Bruce D. Perry and Maia Szalavitz, *The Boy Who Was Raised as a Dog* (New York: Hachette Book Group, 2017); Robert Sapolsky, *Why Zebras Don't Get Ulcers* (New York: Freeman Press, 1999); Jack Shonkoff, "Leveraging the Biology of Adversity to Address the Roots of Disparities in Health and Development," *Proceedings of the National Academy of Sciences of the United States of America* 109, suppl. 2 (2012): 17302–17307, https://doi.org/10.1073/pnas.1121259109; Leonard A. Syme, "Social Determinants of Health: The Community as an Empowered Partner," *Preventing Chronic Disease* 1, no. 1 (2004): A02; Nance Wilson et al., "Getting to Social Action: The Youth Empowerment Strategies (YES!) Project," *Health Promotion Practice* 9, no. 4 (2008): 395–403, doi:10.1177/1524839906289072. Philoxene, David. "'Can You Feel Me . . .'"

26. *Unnatural Causes.*

27. Abraham Maslow, "A Theory of Human Motivation," *Psychological Review* 50 (1943): 370–96.

28. *Unnatural Causes.*

29. David Williams, as quoted in *Unnatural Causes.*

30. Bruce S. McEwen and Teresa Seeman, "Protective and Damaging Effects of Mediators of Stress: Elaborating and Testing the Concepts of Allostasis and Allostatic Load," *Annals of the New York Academy of Science* 896, no. 1 (1999):30–47. doi: 10.1111/j.1749-6632.1999.tb08103.x. PMID: 10681886.

31. *Unnatural Causes*; Arline T. Geronimus et al., "'Weathering' and Age Patterns of Allostatic Load Scores among Blacks and Whites in the United States," *American Journal of Public Health* 96, no. 5 (2006): 826–33; McEwen and Seeman, "Protective and Damaging Effects."

32. McEwen and Seeman, "Protective and Damaging Effects."

33. Geronimus et al., "'Weathering.'"

34. Sapolsky, *Why Zebras Don't Get Ulcers*; *Unnatural Causes.*

35. Jerry Tello, *Recovering Your Sacredness* (Hacienda Heights, CA: Sueños Publications LLC, 2019).

36. Chester M. Pierce, "Psychiatric Problems of the Black Minority," in *American Handbook of Psychiatry,* ed. Silvano Arieti (New York: Basic Books, 1974), 512–23, quoted in Daniel Solórzano, Miguel Ceja, and Tara Yosso, "Critical Race Theory, Racial Microaggressions, and Campus Racial Climate: The Experiences of African American College Students," *Journal of Negro Education* 69, nos. 1/2 (2000): 60.

37. Solórzano, Ceja, and Yosso, "Critical Race Theory," 60.

38. Antwi A. Akom, "Ameritocracy and Infra-Racial Racism: Racializing Social and Cultural Reproduction Theory in the Twenty-First Century," *Race, Ethnicity, and Education* 11, no. 3 (2008): 205–30; *Unnatural Causes*; Geronimus, et al., "Weath-

ering"; Kevin L. Nadal, *Microaggressions and Traumatic Stress: Theory, Research, and Clinical Treatment* (Washington, DC: American Psychological Association, 2018); David R. Williams, "The Health of U.S. Racial and Ethnic Populations," *Journals of Gerontology* B 60, Special Issue 2 (2005): 53–62.

39. *Unnatural Causes.*
40. *Unnatural Causes.*
41. Tracy Fernandez Rysavy, "Our Interview with Van Jones," August 31, 2021, https://www.greenamerica.org/greed-green/our-interview-van-jones.
42. Akom, "Eco-Apartheid," 836.
43. Akom, "Ameritocracy," 211.
44. Akom, "Ameritocracy," 211.
45. Nadine Burke Harris, *The Deepest Well: Healing the Long-Term Effects of Childhood Adversity* (New York: Mariner Books, 2019); Perry and Szalavitz, *Boy Who Was Raised as a Dog*; Bessel van der Kolk, *The Body Keeps the Score: Brain, Mind, and Body in the Healing of Trauma* (New York: Penguin, 2015).
46. Jill Tucker, "Children Who Survive Urban Warfare Suffer from PTSD, Too," *San Francisco Gate*, 1–7. August 26, 2007.
47. Robert Prentice, quoted in *Unnatural Causes.*
48. Jack Shonkoff, quoted in *Unnatural Causes.*
49. Victor G. Carrion, Carl F. Weems, and Allan L. Reiss, "Stress Predicts Brain Changes in Children: A Pilot Longitudinal Study on Youth Stress, Posttraumatic Stress Disorder, and the Hippocampus," *Pediatrics* 119, no. 3 (2007): 509–16; Hilit Kletter, Carl F. Weems, and Victor G. Carrion, "Guilt and Posttraumatic Stress Symptoms in Child Victims of Interpersonal Violence," *Journal of Clinical Child Psychology and Psychiatry* 14, no. 1 (2009): 71–83.
50. Victor Carrion, as quoted in Tucker, "Children Who Survive."
51. Mindy Thompson Fullilove, *Root Shock: How Tearing Up City Neighborhoods Hurts America, and What We Can Do About It* (New York: New Village Press, 2004), 11.
52. *Unnatural Causes*; Ann Milne, *Coloring in the White Spaces: Reclaiming Cultural Identity in Whitestream Schools* (New York: Peter Lang, 2016).
53. *Unnatural Causes.*
54. Jack Shonkoff, quoted in *Unnatural Causes.*
55. "Japan 'The Most Healthy Country,'" *BBC News*, June 5, 2000, http://news.bbc.co.uk/2/hi/health/774434.stm; *Unnatural Causes.*
56. Christopher Murray, quoted in "Japan," 2.
57. Murray, quoted in "Japan."
58. *Unnatural Causes.*
59. Akom, "Ameritocracy."
60. "Competing Theories of Cholera," UCLA Department of Epidemiology, Fielding School of Public Health, http://www.ph.ucla.edu/epi/snow/choleratheories.html.
61. Bryan Stevenson, "The U.S. Should Take Germany's Lead on Facing Down a Violent History," *NowThis Opinions*, July 21, 2019, season 2, episode 116, https://nowthisnews.com/videos/news/the-us-should-take-germanys-lead-on-facing-down-a-violent-history.
62. Stevenson, "The U.S. Should Take Germany's Lead."
63. Stevenson.

CHAPTER 3

1. Sarah Treuhaft, Angela Glover Blackwell, and Manuel Pastor, *America's Future: Equity Is the Superior Growth Model* (PolicyLink, with University of Southern California's Program for Environmental and Regional Equity, November 2011), https://www.policylink.org/sites/default/files/SUMMIT_FRAMING_WEB_20120110.PDF.

2. Danny Dorling, *The Equality Effect* (Oxford: The New Internationalist, 2017), 13.

3. Langston Hughes, *The Collected Poems of Langston Hughes* (London: Vintage Classics, 1995), 426.

4. Martin Luther King, Jr., "I Have a Dream" (speech, Washington, DC, August 28, 1963).

5. Abraham Maslow, "A Theory of Human Motivation," *Psychological Review* 50 (1943): 6.

6. Ryan Heavy Head and Narcisse Blood, *Naamitapiikoan: Blackfoot Influences on Abraham Maslow's Developmental and Organizational Psychology* (Alexandria, VA: Microtraining Associates, 2011).

7. Heavy Head and Blood, *Naamitapiikoan.*

8. Heavy Head and Blood.

9. Steve Taylor, "Original Influences. How the Ideals of America and Psychology Itself Were Shaped by Native Americans," *Psychology Today*, March 22, 2019, p. 1, https://www.psychologytoday.com/us/blog/out-the-darkness/201903/original-influences.

10. Edward Hoffman, *Future Visions: The Unpublished Papers of Abraham Maslow* (London: Sage, 1996).

11. Cindy Blackstock, "When Everything Matters: What Happens to Children When They Are Brought into Care?" lecture, 32nd Annual National Indian Child Welfare Association Conference, Fort Lauderdale, FL, 2014.

12. Taylor, "Original Influences," 2019.

13. Ronald Wright, *Stolen Continents* (Boston: Houghton Mifflin, 1992), 1.

14. Patrick Camangian, "Starting with Self: Teaching Autoethnography to Foster Critically Caring Literacies," *Research in the Teaching of English* 45, no. 2 (2010): 179–204; Jeff Duncan-Andrade, "Note to Educators: Hope Required When Growing Roses in Concrete," *Harvard Education Review* 79, no. 2 (2009): 1–13; Mariella Espinoza-Herold, "Introducing Carla: 'This Is America and Here You Speak English!'," in Mariella Espinoza-Herold and Ricardo González-Carriedo, *Issues in Latino Education: Race, School Culture, and the Politics of Academic Success* (Boston: Allyn and Bacon, 2003), 67–93; Nel Noddings, *Caring: A Feminine Approach to Ethics and Moral Education*, 2nd ed. (Berkeley: University of California Press, 1984, 2013; citations refer to the 2013 edition); Angela Valenzuela, *Subtractive Schooling: U.S.-Mexican Youth and the Politics of Caring* (Albany: State University of New York Press, 1999); Herbert Kohl, *I Won't Learn from You* (New York: New Press, 1995).

15. Cindy Blackstock, "Emergence of the Breath of Life Theory," *Journal of Social Work Values and Ethics* 8, no. 1 (2011): 1–16; Terry L. Cross et al., "Defining Youth Success Using Culturally Appropriate Community-Based Participatory Research Methods," *Best Practices in Mental Health* 7, no. 1 (2011): 94–114; Leonard S. Syme, "Social Determinants of Health: The Community as an Empowered Partner," *Preventing Chronic Disease* 1, no. 1 (2004): A02; Nadine Burke Harris,

The Deepest Well: Healing the Long-Term Effects of Childhood Adversity (New York: Mariner Books, 2019); Bruce Perry and Maia Szalavitz, *The Boy Who Was Raised as a Dog* (New York, Hachette Books, 2017*)*; Jerry Tello, *Recovering Your Sacredness* (Hacienda Heights, CA: Sueños Publications LLC, 2019); Shawn Ginwright, *Black Youth Rising* (New York: Teachers College Press, 2009); Shawn Ginwright, *Hope and Healing in Urban Education* (New York: Routledge Press, 2015); Bessel van der Kolk, *The Body Keeps the Score: Brain, Mind, and Body in the Healing of Trauma* (New York: Penguin, 2015); Mark Brackett, *Permission to Feel* (New York: Celadon Books, 2019).

16. Tara J. Yosso, "Whose Culture Has Capital? A Critical Race Theory Discussion of Community Cultural Wealth," *Race Ethnicity and Education* 8, no. 1 (2005): 69–91.

17. Camangian, "Starting with Self"; Duncan-Andrade, "Note to Educators"; Jeff Duncan-Andrade and Ernest Morrell, *The Art of Critical Pedagogy* (New York: Peter Lang, 2008); Paulo Freire, *Pedagogy of the Oppressed* (New York: Continuum, 1970); Paulo Freire, *Pedagogy of Hope* (London: Bloomsbury Academic, 2014); Bettina Love, *We Want to Do More than Survive: Abolitionist Teaching and the Pursuit of Educational Freedom* (Boston: Beacon Press, 2019); Ann Milne, *Coloring in the White Spaces: Reclaiming Cultural Identity in Whitestream Schools* (New York: Peter Lang, 2016); Tello, *Recovering Your Sacredness;* Samuel Martinez, *Amerikkaka* (Bloomington, IN: AuthorHouse, 2013); Allyson Tintiangco-Cubales and Jeff Duncan-Andrade, "Still Fighting for Ethnic Studies: The Origins, Practices, and Potential of Community Responsive Pedagogy," *Teachers College Record* 123, no. 13 (2021).

18. Gloria Ladson-Billings and William F. Tate IV, "Toward a Critical Race Theory of Education," *Teachers College Record* 97, no. 1 (1995): 47–68.

19. Malcolm X, "Oxford Union Debate" (December 3, 1964), http://malcolmxfiles .blogspot.com/2013/07/oxford-union-debate-december-3-1964.html, posted August 31, 2021.

20. Catherine Clinton, *Harriet Tubman: The Road to Freedom* (New York: Back Bay Books, 2005), 32.

21. Camangian, "Starting with Self."

22. Treuhaft, Blackwell, and Pastor, *America's Future.*

23. Tupac Shakur, *The Rose That Grew from Concrete* (New York: MTV Books, 2006).

24. Shakur, *The Rose That Grew from Concrete.*

25. Ruby Payne, *A Framework for Understanding Poverty* (Highlands, TX: aha! Process, 2005); Abigail Thernstrom and Stephan Thernstrom, *No Excuses: Closing the Racial Gap in Learning* (New York: Simon & Schuster, 2004); John Ogbu and Astrid Davis, *Black American Students in an Affluent Suburb* (Mahwah, NJ: Lawrence Erlbaum Associates, 2003); Dinesh D'Souza, *The End of Racism: Principles for a Multiracial Society* (New York: Free Press, 1995); Richard Herrnstein and Charles Murray, *The Bell Curve* (New York: Free Press, 1994).

26. Jeff Duncan-Andrade, "Gangstas, Wankstas, and Ridas: Defining, Developing, and Supporting Effective Teachers in Urban Schools," *International Journal of Qualitative Studies in Education* 20, no. 6 (2007): 617–638; Duncan-Andrade and Morrell, *Art of Critical Pedagogy*; Duncan-Andrade, "Note to Educators."

27. Duncan-Andrade, "Note to Educators."

CHAPTER 4

1. Angela Valenzuela, *Subtractive Schooling: U.S.-Mexican Youth and the Politics of Caring* (Albany: State University of New York Press, 1999); Herbert Kohl, *I Won't Learn from You* (New York: New Press, 1995); Jeff Duncan-Andrade, "Gangstas, Wankstas, and Ridas: Defining, Developing, and Supporting Effective Teachers in Urban Schools," *International Journal of Qualitative Studies in Education* 20, no. 6 (2007): 617–638; Gloria Ladson-Billings, *The Dreamkeepers: Successful Teachers of African American Children* (San Francisco: Jossey-Bass, 2009); Nel Noddings, *Caring: A Feminine Approach to Ethics and Moral Education*, 2nd ed. (Berkeley: University of California Press, 1984, 2013; citations refer to the 2013 edition unless 1984 is specified); Guadalupe Valdés, *Con Respeto* (New York: Teachers College Press, 1996); Allyson Tintiangco-Cubales and Jeff Duncan-Andrade, "Still Fighting for Ethnic Studies: The Origins, Practices, and Potential of Community Responsive Pedagogy," *Teachers College Record* 123, no. 13 (2021).
2. Kohl, *I Won't Learn from You.*
3. Kohl, 27.
4. Kohl, 2.
5. Kohl.
6. Kohl, 32.
7. David Philoxene, "'Can You Feel Me . . .': The Sociospatial Logics and Ghost-Map of Black and Urban Youth Navigating Urban Violence" (PhD diss., University of California, Berkeley, 2021).
8. Kohl, 29.
9. Noddings, *Caring.*
10. Nel Noddings, *Starting at Home: Caring and Social Policy* (Berkeley: University of California Press, 2002), 23–24.
11. Noddings, *Caring.*
12. Noddings, 24.
13. Noddings, quoted in Valenzuela, *Subtractive Schooling*, 22.
14. Paulo Freire, *Pedagogy of the Oppressed* (New York: Continuum, 1970); see also Cindy Blackstock, "Emergence of the Breath of Life Theory," *Journal of Social Work Values and Ethics* 8, no. 1 (2011): 1–16.
15. Valenzuela, *Subtractive Schooling*, 22.
16. Valenzuela, 23.
17. Valenzuela, 25.
18. Robert Sapolsky, *Why Zebras Don't Get Ulcers* (New York: Freeman Press, 1999).
19. Dena Simmons, "Why SEL Alone Isn't Enough," *ASCD*, March 1, 2021, https://www.ascd.org/el/articles/why-sel-alone-isnt-enough; Tiffani Marie Johnson, "Artelia Green's & Olivia Williams' Legacy: A Study on the Pedagogical Practices that Improve Health for Black Children" (unpublished PhD diss., University of California, Berkeley, 2020); Shawn Ginwright, *Hope and Healing in Urban Education* (New York: Routledge Press, 2015); Bruce Perry and Maia Szalavitz, *The Boy Who Was Raised as a Dog* (New York: Hachette Books, 2017); Garber Maté, *When the Body Says No: Understanding the Stress-Disease Connection* (New York: Wiley, 2011); Nadine Burke Harris, *The Deepest Well: Healing the Long-Term Effects of Childhood Adversity* (New York: Mariner Books, 2018); Bessel van der Kolk, *The Body Keeps the*

Score: Brain, Mind, and Body in the Healing of Trauma (New York: Penguin, 2015); Jerry Tello, *Recovering Your Sacredness* (Hacienda Heights, CA: Sueños Publications LLC, 2019); Mark Brackett, *Permission to Feel* (New York: Celadon Books, 2019); Resmaa Menakem, *My Grandmother's Hands* (Las Vegas, NV: Central Recovery Press, 2017).

20. *Unnatural Causes*, directed by Llewellyn Smith, California Newsreel, 2008, https://www.pbs.org/unnaturalcauses/about_the_series.htm.

21. Burke Harris, *Deepest Well*.

22. Burke Harris, 90.

23. Burke Harris, 90; van der Kolk, *Body Keeps the Score*; Perry and Szalavitz, *Boy Who Was Raised as a Dog*.

24. Johnson, "Artelia Green's & Olivia Williams' Legacy"; Sharim Hannegan-Martinez, "Literacies of Love: Trauma, Healing, and Pedagogical Shifts in an English Classroom" (PhD diss., University of California, Los Angeles, 2020); Ladson-Billings, *Dreamkeepers*; Menakem, *Grandmother's Hands*; Julio Cammarota and Augustine Romero, *The Public Option for Educational Revolution* (Tucson: University of Arizona Press, 2014); Antonia Darder, *Reinventing Paulo Freire: A Pedagogy of Love* (New York: Routledge Press, 2017); Leonard A. Syme, "Social Determinants of Health: The Community as an Empowered Partner," *Preventing Chronic Disease* 1, no. 1 (2004): A02; Charles R. Snyder, "Hope Theory: Rainbows in the Mind," *Psychological Inquiry* 13, no. 2 (2002): 249–275; Jeff Duncan-Andrade, "Note to Educators: Hope Required When Growing Roses in Concrete," *Harvard Education Review* 79 no. 2 (2009): 1–13; Ginwright, *Hope and Healing*.

25. Syme, "Social Determinants of Health."

26. Syme, 3.

27. Syme.

28. *Unnatural Causes*.

29. Johnson, "Artelia Green's & Olivia Williams' Legacy"; Burke Harris, *Deepest Well*; Perry and Szalavitz, *Boy Who Was Raised as a Dog*; Tello, *Recovering Your Sacredness*. 2019.

30. Johnson, "Artelia Green's & Olivia Williams' Legacy"; Burke Harris, *Deepest Well*; Perry and Szalavitz, *Boy Who Was Raised as a Dog*; Beverly Daniel Tatum, *Why Are All the Black Kids Sitting Together in the Cafeteria?* (New York: Basic Books, 1997); Tello, *Recovering Your Sacredness*.

31. Valenzuela, *Subtractive Schooling*, Duncan-Andrade, "Note to Educators"; Shawn Ginwright, *Black Youth Rising* (New York: Teachers College Press, 2009); Ginwright, *Hope and Healing*.

32. Sukhdip Boparai et al., "Adversity and Academic Performance among Adolescent Youth: A Community-Based Participatory Research Study," *Journal of Adolescent and Family Health* 8, no. 1 (2017): 1–33; Allyson Tintiangco-Cubales and Jocyl Sacramento, "Practicing Pinayist Pedagogy," *Amerasia Journal* 35, no. 1 (2009): 179–87; Cammarota and Romero, *The Public Option*; Noddings, *Caring*; Kohl, *I Won't Learn from You*; Lisa Delpit, *Other People's Children: Cultural Conflict in the Classroom* (New York: New Press, 1995); Lisa Delpit and Joanne K. Dowdy, *The Skin That We Speak* (New York: New Press, 2002); Valenzuela, *Subtractive Schooling*; Duncan-Andrade, "Gangstas, Wankstas, and Ridas"; Jeff Duncan-Andrade

and Ernest Morrell, *The Art of Critical Pedagogy* (New York: Peter Lang, 2008); Duncan-Andrade, "Note to Educators"; Jeff Duncan-Andrade, *What a Coach Can Teach a Teacher: Lessons Urban Schools Can Learn from a Successful Sports Program* (New York: Peter Lang, 2010); Tyrone C. Howard, *Black Male(d)* (New York: Teachers College Press, 2013); Richard Milner, *Rac(e)ing to Class* (Boston: Harvard Education Press, 2015); Pedro A. Noguera, *City Schools and the American Dream: Reclaiming the Promise of Public Education* (New York: Teachers College Press, 2003); Pedro A. Noguera, *The Trouble with Black Boys: And Other Reflections on Race, Equity, and the Future of Public Education* (San Francisco: Jossey-Bass, 2008).

33. Brené Brown, "The Power of Vulnerability," TED Talk, TEDxHouston, June 2010, https://www.ted.com/talks/brene_brown_the_power_of_vulnerability?language=en.

34. Brené Brown, *Daring Greatly* (New York: Avery, 2012).

35. Brown, "Power of Vulnerability."

36. Theresa Wiseman, "A Concept Analysis of Empathy," *Journal of Advanced Nursing* 23, (1996): 1163.

37. Wiseman, 1165.

38. Jason Thompson, "The Science of Youth Trauma and Community Responsive Pedagogy," presentation, Community Responsive Education Fall Symposium, Oakland, CA, August 2018.

39. Brown, *Daring Greatly*; Brown, "Vulnerability."

40. Brown, *Daring Greatly*.

41. Jason M. Thompson, *Atlantis: A Memoir* (New York: Harper Collins, forthcoming); Tatum, *Sitting Together in the Cafeteria*; Brown, *Daring Greatly*; Menakem, *My Grandmother's Hands*; Perry and Szalavitz, *Boy Who Was Raised as a Dog*; Burke Harris, *Deepest Well*; van der Kolk, *Body Keeps the Score*; Sapolsky, *Why Zebras Don't Get Ulcers*.

42. Menakem, *My Grandmother's Hands*; Robin DiAngelo, *White Fragility: Why It's So Hard for White People to Talk About Racism* (Boston: Beacon Press, 2018).

43. Menakem, *My Grandmother's Hands*, xviii.

44. I know of only five schools that have made the dismantling of white supremacy their primary objective: Kia Aroha (New Zealand), Roses in Concrete Community School (Oakland, California), Semillas del Pueblo (Los Angeles, California), Chula Vista Learning Community Center (San Diego, California), and Ile Omode (Oakland, California).

45. Simmons, "Why SEL Alone Isn't Enough."

46. David Tyack and Larry Cuban, *Tinkering Toward Utopia* (Boston: Harvard University Press, 1997); DiAngelo, *White Fragility*.

47. Perry and Szalavitz, *Boy Who Was Raised as a Dog*, 267-268.

48. Perry and Szalavitz, 268.

49. Maestro Tello is a founder of the National Compadres Network (https://www.nationalcompadresnetwork.org/training/lcc-overview/) whose work with children and families around the country is some of the most profound, impactful, and important that I have seen anywhere in the world.

50. Perry and Szalavitz, *Boy Who Was Raised as a Dog*, 274.

51. Tello, *Recovering Your Sacredness*, 23–24.

52. Tintiangco-Cubales and Duncan-Andrade, "Still Fighting for Ethnic Studies."

53. A special thanks here to my dear friend and comrade, Dr. Patrick Camangian, who introduced me to this powerful file: *Children Full of Life*, directed by Noboru Kaetsu, documentary film, Japan NHK, 2013. The film begins in the second year of a two-year loop for Kanamori and his students. That is, Kanamori was this class's teacher the year before in third grade. The filmmakers do not make much of this fact, but as a teacher who looped my entire career, I am certain the depth of relationships we see in the film is related to this fact. This does not in any way diminish the skill of Kanamori as a teacher. If he were an ineffective teacher in year one of the loop, we would have seen the collateral damage of those failures all over the film.

54. *Children Full of Life*, at Top Documentary Films, https://topdocumentaryfilms.com/children-full-of-life/.

55. This concept of "hope dealer" was first presented to me by Tiffani Marie Johnson, one of the most brilliant teachers, researchers, and artists I know. Some of her work is cited throughout the book, and I go into depth as one of the practice-based examples in chapter 6.

56. This accounting of the work going on at Lincoln High School (Washington) draws heavily from the reporting of Jane Ellen Stevens and the documentary film *Paper Tigers*. Jane E. Stevens, "Lincoln High School in Walla Walla, WA, Tries New Approach to School Discipline—Suspensions Drop 85%," ACEs Too High News, April 23, 2012, https://acestoohigh.com/2012/04/23/lincoln-high-school-in-walla-walla-wa-tries-new-approach-to-school-discipline-expulsions-drop-85/; *Paper Tigers*, directed by James Redford, documentary film, KPJR Films, 2015, https://kpjrfilms.co/paper-tigers/.

57. Stevens, "Lincoln High School," 2.

58. John Medina. *Brain Rules* (New York: Pear Press, 2017).

59. Stevens.

60. Stevens.

61. Stevens, 5.

62. According to Stevens ("Lincoln High School"), Turner's model is based on the ARC (Attachment, Regulation, Competency) model, which was developed at the Trauma Center at the Justice Resource Institute. Turner's team has also drawn from Susan F. Cole et al., *Helping Traumatized Children Learn* (Boston: Massachusetts Advocates for Children, 2005).

63. Stevens, "Lincoln High School," 5.

64. Stevens, 6.

65. Tello, *Recovering Your Sacredness*, Perry and Szalavitz, *Boy Who Was Raised as a Dog*.

66. Perry and Szalavitz, *Boy Who Was Raised as a Dog*, 274–75.

67. See Perry and Szalavitz's story (*Boy Who Was Raised as a Dog*) about Mama P and her "intuitive" approach to healing children. See also Johnson, "Artelia Green's & Olivia Williams' Legacy" and Menakem, *My Grandmother's Hands*.

68. Perry and Szalavitz, *Boy Who Was Raised as a Dog*, 260–61.

CHAPTER 5

1. Thomas Dee and Emily Penner, "The Causal Effects of Cultural Relevance: Evidence from an Ethnic Studies Curriculum" (Stanford University Center for Education Policy Analysis (CEPA) Working Paper 2016: 16–01); Abraham Maslow,

"A Theory of Human Motivation," *Psychological Review* 50 (1943): 370–96; Jeff Duncan-Andrade, "Utilizing *Cariño* in the Development of Research Methodologies," in *The Praeger Handbook of Urban Education*, ed. Joe L. Kincheloe et al. (Westport, CT: Greenwood Publishing Group, 2006), 451–86; Claude M. Steele, *Whistling Vivaldi* (New York: W. W. Norton, 2011); Robert Rosenthal and Lenore Jacobson, *Pygmalion in the Classroom* (Carmarthen, UK: Crown House, 2003); Carol S. Dweck, *Mindset: The New Psychology of Success* (New York: Ballantine Books, 2006).

2. Maslow, "Human Motivation."

3. Leonard A. Syme, "Social Determinants of Health: The Community as an Empowered Partner," *Preventing Chronic Disease* 1, no. 1 (2004): A02; Charles R. Snyder, "Hope Theory: Rainbows in the Mind," *Psychological Inquiry* 13, no. 2 (2002): 249–75; Jeff Duncan-Andrade, "Note to Educators: Hope Required When Growing Roses in Concrete," *Harvard Education Review* 79 no. 2 (2009): 1–13.

4. Steele, *Whistling Vivaldi*.

5. Dweck, *Mindset*.

6. *Cultural relevance:* Gloria Ladson-Billings, *The Dreamkeepers: Successful Teachers of African American Children* (San Francisco: Jossey-Bass, 2009); *cultural responsiveness:* Zaretta L. Hammond, *Culturally Responsive Teaching and the Brain* (New York: Corwin, 2014); *cultural sustainability:* Django Paris and H. Samy Alim, *Culturally Sustaining Pedagogies: Teaching and Learning for Justice in a Changing World* (New York: Teachers College Press, 2017).

7. Allyson Tintiangco-Cubales and Jeff Duncan-Andrade, "Still Fighting for Ethnic Studies: The Origins, Practices, and Potential of Community Responsive Pedagogy," *Teachers College Record* 123, no. 13 (2021).

8. Joel Spring, *Deculturalization and the Struggle for Equality* (New York: McGraw-Hill, 2001), 27).

9. Spring, *Deculturalization*, 26–27.

10. Spring, 27.

11. Spring.

12. Carter G. Woodson, *The Mis-Education of the Negro* (New York: Classic House Books, 1933).

13. Beverly Daniel Tatum, *Why Are All the Black Kids Sitting Together in the Cafeteria?* (New York: Basic Books, 1997); William H. Watkins, *The White Architects of Black Education* (New York: Teachers College Press, 2001); Tiffani Marie Johnson, "Artelia Green's & Olivia Williams' Legacy: A Study on the Pedagogical Practices that Improve Health for Black Children" (unpublished PhD diss., University of California, Berkeley, 2020); Michael J. Dumas, "'Losing an Arm': Schooling as a Site of Black Suffering," *Race Ethnicity and Education* 17, no. 1 (2014): 1–29, doi: 10.1080/13613324.20:3.850412; Bettina Love, *We Want to Do More than Survive: Abolitionist Teaching and the Pursuit of Educational Freedom* (Boston: Beacon Press, 2019); Michelle Alexander, *The New Jim Crow* (New York: The New Press, 2012).

14. Angela Valenzuela, *Subtractive Schooling: U.S.-Mexican Youth and the Politics of Caring* (Albany: State University of New York Press, 1999); Jeff Duncan-Andrade, "An Examination of the Sociopolitical History of Chicanos and Its Relationship to School Performance," *Urban Education* 40, no. 6 (2005): 576–605; Rodolfo F.

Acuña, *Occupied America: A History of Chicanos* (San Francisco: Pearson, 2014); Antonia Darder, Rodolfo D. Torres, and Henry Gutiérrez, *Latinos and Education* (New York: Taylor and Francis, 1997); Julio Cammarota and Augustine Romero, eds., *Raza Studies: The Public Option for Educational Revolution* (Tucson: University of Arizona Press, 2014); Ann Milne, *Coloring in the White Spaces: Reclaiming Cultural Identity in Whitestream Schools* (New York: Peter Lang, 2016); Allyson Tintiangco-Cubales and Jocyl Sacramento, "Practicing Pinayist Pedagogy," *Amerasia Journal* 35, no. 1 (2009): 179–87; Stacey J. Lee, *Unraveling the "Model Minority" Stereotype: Listening to Asian American Youth* (New York: Teachers College Press, 1996); E.J.R. David, *Brown Skin, White Minds: Filipino-/American Postcolonial Psychology* (Charlotte, NC: Information Age Publishing, 2013); Dawn Mabalon, *Little Manila Is in the Heart: The Making of the Filipina/o American Community in Stockton, California* (Durham, NC: Duke University Press, 2013).
15. Tintiangco-Cubales and Duncan-Andrade, "Still Fighting for Ethnic Studies."
16. Dee and Penner, "Causal Effects of Cultural Relevance."
17. Samuel Bowles and Herbert Gintis, *Schooling in Capitalist America: Educational Reform and the Contradictions of Economic Life* (New York: Basic Books, 1976).
18. Allyson Tintiangco-Cubales et al., "Toward an Ethnic Studies Pedagogy: Implications for K–12 Schools from the Research," *Urban Review* 47 (2014): doi:2014 10.1007/s11256-014-0280-y.
19. John Dewey, *The Child and the Curriculum* (Chicago: University of Chicago Press, 1902).
20. Nance Wilson et al., "Getting to Social Action: The Youth Empowerment Strategies (YES!) Project," *Health Promotion Practice* 9, no. 4 (2008): 395–403, doi:10.1177/1524839906289072; Syme, "Social Determinants of Health."
21. Syme, "Social Determinants of Health," 3.
22. Snyder, "Hope Theory," Lisa A. Edwards, Anthony D. Ong, and Shane J. Lopez, "Hope Measurement in Mexican American Youth," *Journal of Behavioral Sciences* 29, no. 2 (2007): 225–41; Philip R. Magaletta and J. M. Oliver, "The Hope Construct, Will, and Ways: Their Relations with Self-Efficacy, Optimism, and General Well-Being," *Journal of Clinical Psychology* 55 (1999): 539–51; Charles R. Snyder et al., "Optimism and Hope Constructs: Variants on a Positive Expectancy Theme," in *Optimism and Pessimism*, ed. E. C. Chang (Washington, DC: American Psychological Association, 2001): 101–25; Charles R. Snyder et al., "The Development and Validation of the Children's Hope Scale," *Journal of Pediatric Psychology* 22 (1997): 399–421.
23. In June 2008, AERA convened a working group to provide a concrete definition of "scientifically based research." The group recently released its definition, which can be found at https://www.aera.net/About-AERA/Key-Programs/Education-Research-Research-Policy/AERA-Offers-Definition-of-Scientifically-Based-Res#:~:text=Supported%20by%20AERA%20Council%2C%20July,obtain%20reliable%20and%20valid%20knowledge; *Unnatural Causes*, directed by Llewellyn Smith, California Newsreel, 2008.
24. Duncan-Andrade, "Note to Educators"; Jeff Duncan-Andrade and Ernest Morrell, *The Art of Critical Pedagogy* (New York: Peter Lang, 2008); Jeff Duncan-Andrade, "Gangstas, Wankstas, and Ridas: Defining, Developing, and Supporting Effective

Teachers in Urban Schools," *International Journal of Qualitative Studies in Education* 20, no. 6 (2007): 617–38.

25. In my 2009 article "Note to Educators: Hope Required When Growing Roses from Concrete," I distinguish between "false hope" and "critical hope." False hope is a reactionary distortion of the radical premise of hope. It appears in three forms in schools: hokey hope, mythical hope, and hope deferred. On the flip side of these false hopes lies "critical hope," which rejects the despair of hopelessness and the false hopes of "cheap American optimism" (Cornel West, *Hope on a Tightrope* (New York: Smiley Books, 2008) 41?. Critical hope demands a committed and active struggle "against the evidence in order to change the deadly tides of wealth inequality, group xenophobia, and personal despair" (Cornel West, "Prisoners of Hope," in *The Impossible Will Take a Little While: A Citizen's Guide to Hope in a Time of Fear*, ed. Paul R. Loeb (New York: Basic Books, 2004), 293–97). There are three elements of critical hope: material, Socratic, and audacious.

26. Heather McGhee, *The Sum of Us* (New York: One World, 2021).

27. Lisa Delpit, *Other People's Children: Cultural Conflict in the Classroom* (New York: New Press, 1995).

28. Shawn Ginwright, *Black Youth Rising* (New York: Teachers College Press, 2009).

29. West, "Prisoners of Hope," 295.

30. West, 296.

31. *Unnatural Causes.*

32. Camara Jones, "Levels of Racism: A Theoretic Framework and a Gardener's Tale, *American Journal of Public Health* 90 (2000): 1213.

33. Tupac Shakur, *The Rose That Grew from Concrete* (New York: MTV Books, 2006).

34. Jeremiah Wright, "The Audacity to Hope," *Preaching Today*, 1990, https://www.preachingtoday.com/sermons/sermons/2010/july/audacityofhope.html

35. Yang has written on this idea of inclusionary practice, creating a framework for classroom discipline that critiques traditional models of school discipline as nothing more than exclusionary models of punishment that are bad for teachers and students; see K. Wayne Yang, "Discipline or Punish? Some Suggestions for School Policy and Teacher Practice" in *Language Arts* 87, no. 1 (2009): 49–61. Retrieved from https://escholarship.org/uc/item/8ss5t567.

36. Jeff Duncan-Andrade, "Gangstas, Wankstas, and Ridas"; Valenzuela, *Subtractive Schooling*; Delpit, *Other People's Children*; Herbert Kohl, *I Won't Learn from You* (New York: New Press, 1995); Ladson-Billings, *The Dreamkeepers*; Sonia Nieto and Patty Bode, *Affirming Diversity: The Sociopolitical Context of Multicultural Education* (New York: Longman, 1992); Nel Noddings, *The Challenge to Care in Schools: An Alternative Approach to Education* (New York: Teachers College Press, 1992).

37. Claude M. Steele and Joshua Aronson, "Stereotype Threat and the Intellectual Test Performance of African Americans," *Journal of Personality and Social Psychology* 69, no. 5 (1995): 797–811.

38. Steven J. Spencer, Claude M. Steele, and Diane M. Quinn, "Stereotype Threat and Women's Math Performance," *Journal of Experimental Social Psychology* 35, no. 1 (1999): 4–28, doi:10.1006/jesp.1998.1373.

39. Jeff Stone et al., "Stereotype Threat Effects on Black and White Athletic Performance," *Journal of Personality and Social Psychology* 77, no. 6 (1999): 1213–27, doi:10.1037/0022-3514.77.6.1213.
40. Robert Rosenthal and Lenore Jacobson, *Pygmalion in the Classroom* (Carmarthen, UK: Crown House, 2003).
41. Rosenthal and Jacobson, *Pygmalion*, 262.
42. Jennifer L. Eberhardt, *Biased* (New York: Viking Press, 2019); Cheryl Staats et al., *State of the Science: Implicit Bias Review 2015*, Kirwan Institute for the Study of Race and Ethnicity, Ohio State University (2015), http://kirwaninstitute.osu.edu/wp-content/uploads/2015/05/2015-kirwan-implicit-bias.pdf.
43. Carol A Tomlinson, *How to Differentiate Instruction in Academically Diverse Classrooms*, 3rd ed. (Alexandria, VA: ASCD Press, 2017).
44. Dweck, *Mindset*.
45. Angela Duckworth, *Grit: The Power of Passion and Perseverance* (New York: Scribner, 2018).
46. Schools committed to wellness do not see grit and mindset as foundational for achievement for obvious reasons that are discussed in this section.
47. Shakur, *The Rose That Grew from Concrete*.
48. Carol Dweck, "Carol Dweck Revisits the 'Growth Mindset,'" commentary, *EducationWeek*, September 22, 2015, https://www.edweek.org/leadership/opinion-carol-dweck-revisits-the-growth-mindset/2015/09.
49. Dweck, "Carol Dweck Revisits the 'Growth Mindset.'"
50. Milne, *Coloring in the White Spaces*.
51. The significant research supporting these components of student development have been discussed at length in this chapter and in chapter 4. The process by which assessments for student progress in these areas were designed by the teachers, school leadership, and community elders is explored in Milne's book *Coloring in the White Spaces*, which is based on the dissertation she wrote to document the practices of the school.
52. The term *ukukura* was literally created by Māori language keepers to describe the relationship between the Tupuranga community and the Roses in Concrete community. The word is made up of two nouns—*kura*, which means school or schools, and *uku*, which is an ally or a supporting tribe, particularly in battle. A group of Māori language experts combined the two to create a word for schools in solidarity in the struggle.
53. Plessy v. Ferguson, 163 U.S. 537 (1896).
54. Brown v. Board of Education of Topeka, 347 U.S. 483 (1954). Very little has changed since. In honor of the fiftieth anniversary of the *Brown* decision, the Harvard Civil Rights Project (now the UCLA Civil Rights Project) released a report evaluating the nation's progress. Their data revealed that schools in all regions outside of the South are more racially segregated now than *before* the *Brown* decision. Nationally, Latinx and African American students are more segregated now than they were in 1968.
55. The implementation of ninth-grade Ethnic Studies classes in San Francisco Unified Schools may change this fact in at least one city.

56. I put the word "American" in quotation marks, because as part of this project of white supremacy, the United States has claimed the title of America, even though we are one of several countries that make up the Americas. So, in fact, Canadians, Mexicans, and every other group from North and South America are actually Americans.
57. My closing thoughts in this chapter borrow heavily from the introduction of a longer piece about the direction I propose for improving education. For the full paper, see Jeff Duncan-Andrade, "A Glass Half Full," Bank Street Occasional Paper Series 27, 2012, https://educate.bankstreet.edu/occasional-paper-series/vol2012/iss27/12/.

CHAPTER 6

1. Herbert Kohl, *I Won't Learn from You* (New York: New Press, 1995)."
2. Paulo Freire, *Pedagogy of the Oppressed* (New York: Continuum, 1970), 44.
3. Freire, *Pedagogy of the Oppressed*,
4. Antonia Darder, *Reinventing Paulo Freire: A Pedagogy of Love* (New York: Routledge, 2017); Jerry Tello, *Recovering Your Sacredness* (Hacienda Heights, CA: Sueños Publications, 2019); Bruce D. Perry and Maia Szalavitz, *The Boy Who Was Raised as a Dog* (New York: Hachette, 2017).
5. Bettina Love, *We Want to Do More than Survive: Abolitionist Teaching and the Pursuit of Educational Freedom* (Boston: Beacon Press, 2019).
6. Love, *We Want to Do More than Survive*, 160.
7. Christina Sharpe, *In the Wake: On Blackness and Being* (Durham, NC: Duke University Press, 2016), 17–18.
8. Anna J Egalite and Brian Kisida, "The Effects of Teacher Match on Students" Academic Perceptions and Attitudes," *Educational Evaluation and Policy Analysis* 40, no. 1 (2018): 59–81.
9. Claire C. Miller, "Does Teacher Diversity Matter in Student Learning?," *New York Times*, September 10, 2018, https://www.nytimes.com/2018/09/10/upshot/teacher-diversity-effect-students-learning.html.
10. James Baldwin, *Nobody Knows My Name* (London: Vintage Press, 2002), 96.
11. James Garbarino, *Raising Children in a Socially Toxic Environment* (San Francisco: Jossey-Bass, 1995); Shawn Ginwright, *Hope and Healing in Urban Education* (New York: Routledge Press, 2015).
12. See the argument put forth in chapter 1 of my book with Ernest Morrell, *The Art of Critical Pedagogy* (New York: Peter Lang, 2008), where we argue that schools cannot be failing if they are doing exactly what they are designed to do.
13. *Unnatural Causes*, directed by Llewellyn Smith, California Newsreel, 2008, https://www.pbs.org/unnaturalcauses/about_the_series.htm.
14. *Radical healing*: see Shawn Ginwright, *Black Youth Rising* (New York: Teachers College Press, 2009); Shawn Ginwright, *Hope and Healing. Critical hope*: see Jeff Duncan-Andrade, "Note to Educators: Hope Required When Growing Roses in Concrete," *Harvard Education Review* 79 no. 2 (2009): 1–13.
15. Joel Spring, *American Education: An Introduction to Social and Political Aspects* (New York: Longman, 1989); Samuel Martinez, *Amerikkka* (Bloomington, IN: AuthorHouse, 2013); William H. Watkins, *The White Architects of Black Education* (New York: Teachers College Press, 2001).

16. See https://communityresponsive.org/.
17. Tello, *Recovering Your Sacredness*.
18. Lisa Delpit, *Other People's Children: Cultural Conflict in the Classroom* (New York: New Press, 1995).
19. Dena Simmons, "Why SEL Alone Isn't Enough in ASCD," ASCD, https://www.ascd.org/el/articles/why-sel-alone-isnt-enough, March 1, 2021.
20. For a more detailed description of H20 and Apocalyptic Ed, see www.h2oprod.org and www.apocalypticeducation.org.
21. Kia Aroha is the New Zealand school committed to indigenous practices of education for their youth that is discussed at the end of chapter 5.
22. PowerSchool is a computerized system used to house and track student records and manage other school-based activities and information.
23. Patrick Camangian, "Starting with Self: Teaching Autoethnography to Foster Critically Caring Literacies," *Research in the Teaching of English* 45, no. 2 (2010): 179–204.
24. The commitment, love, and skill that it took to support Reina to write that poem and then to find the courage to perform it in front of our class was largely made possible by another one of my students who, at the time, was one of five teacher apprentices in our class. She and Reina formed a close and deeply caring relationship over time, and it was that relationship, the relevance of the curriculum we were using, and the deep sense of responsibility to create space for the woundedness of our community to find the light of day that opened new possibilities for individual and collective healing. That teaching apprentice went on to teach several years in the community and recently completed her doctoral studies. She is now a teacher of teachers whose own scholarship profoundly expands on discussions in this book. See Sharim Hannegan-Martinez, "Literacies of Love: Trauma, Healing, and Pedagogical Shifts in an English Classroom" (PhD diss., University of California, Los Angeles, 2020). Special thanks also to Dr. Patrick Camangian, who transcribed this poem and was gracious enough to share it with me.

CHAPTER 7

1. Angela Valenzuela, *Subtractive Schooling: U.S.-Mexican Youth and the Politics of Caring* (Albany: State University of New York Press, 1999).
2. Anand Giridharadas, *Winners Take All: The Elite Charade of Changing the World* (New York: Knopf, 2018).
3. David Tyack, *The One Best System: A History of American Urban Education* (Cambridge, MA: Harvard University Press, 1974).
4. Peter L. McLaren and James M. Giarelli, "Introduction: Critical Theory and Educational Research," in *Critical Theory and Educational Research*, ed. Peter L. McLaren and James M. Giarelli (New York: SUNY Press, 1995), 1–22.
5. Linda Tuhiwai-Smith, *Decolonizing Methodologies: Research and Indigenous Peoples* (New York: Zed Books, 1999).
6. Freire (2014), Paulo Freire. *Pedagogy of Hope.* (London: Bloomsbury Academic, 2014), 8.
7. My framing of the changes needed in teacher education are largely taken from a piece I wrote entitled "The Principal Facts." Jeffrey M. R. Duncan-Andrade, "The

Principal Facts: New Directions for Teacher Education," in *Studying Diversity in Teacher Education*, ed. Arnetha F. Ball and Cynthia A. Tyson (New York: Rowman & Littlefield, 2011).

8. It should be noted that there are a growing number of scholars in schools of education (many of whom are faculty of color) who continue to teach in urban schools while maintaining tenure-track faculty positions. Most of these faculty members do this work with little to no additional university support, an issue that should be taken up with universities that espouse a commitment to vulnerable communities.

9. For examples, see Gloria Ladson-Billings, *The Dreamkeepers* (San Francisco: Jossey-Bass, 1992; rep. 2009); Jeff Duncan-Andrade, "Gangstas, Wankstas, and Ridas: Defining, Developing, and Supporting Effective Teachers in Urban Schools," *International Journal of Qualitative Studies in Education* 20, no. 6 (2007): 617–38.

10. A collection of scholars from San Francisco State, including myself, developed an urban teacher quality index tool that draws from leading research to identify the characteristics of effective urban teachers, but is also context sensitive by responding to input from key local stakeholders (students, families, administrators, and educators). Similar efforts could be undertaken inside of any teacher education program to establish core, local criteria for identifying and selecting mentor teachers.

11. Karen H. Quartz, Brad Olsen, and Jeff Duncan-Andrade, "The Fragility of Urban Teaching: A Longitudinal Study of Career Development and Activism," in *Partnering to Prepare Urban Teachers: A Call to Activism,* ed. Francine Peterman (New York: Peter Lang, 2008), 225–48.

12. Robert Greenleaf, *Servant Leadership* (New York: Paulist Press, 2002); Carter G. Woodson, *The Mis-Education of the Negro* (New York: Classic House Books, 1933; rep. 2008), 96.

13. "The Definite Dozen," in Jeff Duncan-Andrade, *What a Coach Can Teach a Teacher: Lessons Urban Schools Can Learn from a Successful Sports Program* (New York: Peter Lang, 2010).

14. Jeff Duncan-Andrade and Ernest Morrell, *The Art of Critical Pedagogy* (New York: Peter Lang, 2008); John Dewey, *Democracy and Education: An Introduction to the Philosophy of Education* (New York: MacMillan, 1904); Woodson, *Mis-Education.*

15. Allyson Tintiangco-Cubales and Jeff Duncan-Andrade, "Still Fighting for Ethnic Studies: The Origins, Practices, and Potential of Community Responsive Pedagogy," *Teachers College Record* 123, no. 13 (2021).

────── ACKNOWLEDGMENTS ──────

This book is dedicated to my suns, Taiyari and Amarú. You breathe new life into my soul every single day. No one has taught me more about unconditional love than the two of you. No one has taught me more about fear than the two of you. We can, and we will, do better for you and your generation. Thank you for all the medicine that you bring into the world. I love you unconditionally.

This book is dedicated to every student I have had the honor of teaching over the last three decades. You allowed me the great privilege to be your teacher. You shared your lives, your hearts, your minds, your stories, your hopes, your dreams, your teachings, and your medicine with me. I apologize for every time I did not show up in the way that you needed me. I am humbled that you were always so willing to let me keep trying and to keep growing alongside of you. I am grateful that so many of you are still part of my life and so generous to me and the boys. I love you unconditionally.

This book is dedicated to all my big homies: Pedro, Gloria, Antonia, Sonia, Carol, and Tío Jerry. You fought for us and our ideas when they were unpopular and denigrated. You created space for us every time they tried to gag us and belittle our dreams and experiences. You sacrificed time with your family, time for your own healing, time that will never be recovered. In your presence, in your cajoling, in your corrections, and in your encouragement, I have always felt seen and loved. Thank you for believing in me and for loving me even when I strayed. I love you unconditionally.

To supporters (Sandra, LaShawn, Jenefer, Lindsay, Giselle, Gaby, and Bethiel) who challenged funders to get behind the kind of work in schools that is argued for in these pages. You took risks and fought for what we believe in, and you did that inside of spaces where voices like ours are far too rare. Your strength and courage are important reminders about what is possible when we support community unapologetically.

This book is dedicated to every parent, educator, and young person who has the courage to dream of a society where our schools promise that our children will be more well when we pick them up than when we dropped them off. Schools that know that this promise is unattainable, but an important one to make nonetheless. Schools that, when they miss that mark, are committed to atoning the very next day by pouring extra medicine into the children with whom they missed the day before. Schools that are keeping track and centering the needs of the most vulnerable and wounded ones every single day. You all are the promise and the possibility that we can finally repurpose schools to make sure that every child that walks through the doors of schools, walks back out more well for their time there. You are living proof that this is possible.

Finally, this book is dedicated to my mother—first teacher, best teacher. I am grateful for all the gifts of grace you have given me over the years. You taught me work ethic, struggle, integrity, faith, patience, responsibility, and the importance of forgiveness for myself and for others. I love you.

JEFFREY M. R. DUNCAN-ANDRADE, PhD, is son to Ada Graciela and the late William Jackson. He is father to Amarú and Taiyari. He is professor of Latina/o Studies and Race and Resistance Studies at San Francisco State University and was one of the founders of the Roses in Concrete Community School, a community responsive lab school in East Oakland (California). As a classroom teacher and school leader in East Oakland for the past twenty-eight years, his pedagogy has been widely studied and acclaimed for producing uncommon levels of social and academic success for students. Duncan-Andrade lectures around the world and has authored numerous journal articles and book chapters on effective practices in schools. In 2016, he was among the great educators invited to the White House on National Teacher Appreciation Day by President Obama, and in 2019 he was chosen as the Laureate for the prestigious Brock International Prize in Education. In 2021, he was selected to join the Board of Prevent Child Abuse America. Duncan-Andrade has also been ranked as one of the nation's most influential scholars by *EdWeek*'s Public Influence Rankings.

Duncan-Andrade's transformational work on the elements of effective teaching in schools is recognized throughout the US and as far abroad as New Zealand. His research interests and publications span the areas of youth wellness, trauma responsiveness, curriculum change, teacher development and retention, critical pedagogy, and cultural and Ethnic Studies. He works closely with teachers, school district and site leaders, union leaders, policy makers, and communities to help them develop practices and cultures that foster self-confidence, esteem, and academic success among all children. Duncan-Andrade holds a PhD in Social and Cultural Studies in Education and a BA in literature, both from the University of California, Berkeley.